Junior Handling

The White Way

Marina White

Dedication

I wish to thank my Mum for all her training over the years, Dad for helping to put the book together, and my brother, Simon, for his continuous support.

Acknowledgements

Thank you for all the junior handlers who submitted case histories: Helena Hutchings, Kelly McWilliams, Annabel Davies, Charlene Kirk, Shona Taylor, Katie Hamilton, Alex Paisey and Mark Mortensen for the photographs. Thanks also to Liz Cartledge for her foreword. Thanks to David Dalton and Sue Domun for help with some of the photography.

Cover photo: Sue Domun.

Edited and Designed by:
International Publishing Associates, Lydney, Glos.

First published in 2002 by Marina White

From March 2002 the KCJO changed its name to the Young Kennel Club (YKC).

ISBN 1 86054 228 X

Printed in Hong Kong through Printworks International Ltd.

10 9 8 7 6 5 4 3 2 1

Contents

Foreword

There has not been a book published on this subject for some years now, so Marina White has certainly got her timing right – in fact, there has never been a book written by an actual junior handler before!

This book is an excellent read, as well as being fully comprehensive, covering all possible aspects of this specialised subject. Marina definitely 'knows her onions' – she started very young and then worked hard to become one of the country's top juniors. She has that natural talent necessary to make it to the top, but she has also had to prove herself and has stayed the course through a combination of talent, determination, and devotion.

At just 19 years old, Marina is now embarking on a career in journalism; I am sure she will apply the same vivacious enthusiasm and boundless energy to writing, as she does to handling her own family's, other people's, show dogs.

This book is full of useful and helpful hints on how to improve your handling skills. The book contains not only Marina's own thoughts, but also those of a whole team of talented young handlers, all fresh, youthful and up-to-the-minute – just like this book.

Attractively illustrated with lots of colour photographs, I am sure this book has everything going for it, and will make a most necessary addition to most juniors' bookshelves.

Liz Cartledge.

Introduction

I was born in Great Yarmouth, Norfolk in 1982 and grew up alongside two Beagles and an over-sized Border Collie. My mother, Margaret, had been involved with Obedience and Working Trial competitions and had handled for many years at dog shows at Exemption, Open and Championship level. Her experience of dogs began in 1971, so you can understand my later involvement and interest.

In my first few years of life I was too preoccupied with my Barbie dolls and teddy bears to understand what dog shows were all about. Then I began

The author, Marina White, with Beagle Peaches.

asking if I could go to some of them with my mother and she was pleased that I was becoming interested in her hobby.

At around six years old I understood the basic routines of breed showing and wanted to have a go myself. My mother lent me our eldest Beagle at that time, Dialynne Purdy of Belsmard (Purdy) to practise handling in the garden. It was only when I felt comfortable handling Purdy that I asked if I could enter a Junior Handling class at the next Open show.

On the day, I tried as hard as I could, eventually gaining a creditable 4th in the 6-11 years class, out of around 20 juniors. Even then my competitive attitude was apparent, as I really would have preferred 1st place.

Looking back at how I began, and at what I have achieved since, is something I am particularly proud of. In 1998, I won the Pedigree Chum UK Junior Handler of the Year Final and then went on to win the Junior Handler World Winner title in Finland. In 1999, I then won the Scottish Junior Handler of the Year Final after being a finalist in the previous two years. At Crufts 2000, I was awarded the Kennel Club Junior Organisation (KCJO) Runner up Show Handler of the Year.

As a result of these wins, I have also written several articles for leading dog newspapers and magazines. Now, at 19 years old, I am pursuing a career in journalism and these articles have given me invaluable writing experience as an introduction to the journalistic world.

The aim of this Junior Handling book is to encourage more youngsters to take up the hobby and also to provide in-depth knowledge of breed handling for the more experienced and mature breeders.

Junior Handling can be an excellent stepping stone into participating and competing against adults in breed competition. It really has helped me to socialise with people of all ages and this has prepared me well for the future.

On a practical note, no gender bias is intended by the convention of using 'he' for both handlers and dogs.

CHAPTER ONE

What is Junior Handling?

In Junior Handling it is the skill of the handler which is being judged, not the dog. This is in marked contrast to breed showing, where the dog is the target of the judge's attention, not the handler.

The System

Children aged between 6 and 16 years of age present their dogs, to the best of their ability, to the judge in a Junior Handling class at a dog show. The Junior Handler will enter the appropriate age class, for example 6-11 years or 12-16 years. The dog being handled must be registered with the Kennel Club and entered in another class at the show (see Chapter 3 – Getting Started).

Executing simple patterns correctly, and a good presentation style, will ensure a well-earned placing in the final line-up. Then, the two class winners compete against each other and the judge will pick one of the handlers to become the Best Junior Handler on the day. This overall winner will be the one who, in the judge's opinion, best demonstrates the ability to emphasise the dog's good points and minimise his faults.

The judge also looks for proficiency in the following areas during the routine round:

- Presentation
- Rapport
- Technique
- Balance

A Junior Handler must impress the judge by trying to get the dog looking his best, both when moving and when standing. So, primarily, this sport teaches youngsters how to handle their dogs correctly which, in turn, can lead them to compete against adults in breed competitions.

Origins of the Sport

This sport began many years ago at exemption shows, where it was not taken particularly seriously, as the winner was often the prettiest little girl in a dress who happened to be holding a dog!

From these humble beginnings, one person in particular decided to take action and set up a suitable organisation in which youngsters could train properly. That person was the late Joe Cartledge and the organisation was called the Dog Centre.

The next stage was to encourage more and more clubs and societies to stage Junior Handling classes by applying through the Dog Centre. They were asked to pay £1, for which they would receive six diplomas, for 1st, 2nd and 3rd in each of the two classes, to give to the winners. These diplomas would qualify the handler to enter the Junior Handling Final, the first of which was held in 1970.

Unfortunately, the Dog Centre did not manage to get off the ground but it became a stepping stone for the creation, in the early 1970s, of the Junior Handling Association that we know today. Sadly, Joe lost his battle with cancer in 1982, but his Swedish-born wife, Liz, has continued being involved with this popular and ever-growing Association.

The Junior Handling Association (JHA)

Nowadays, the scheme works roughly on the original principles, except that the diplomas, which are on offer at most Open and Championship shows, qualify the handler for the Semi-finals held at the Richmond Championship Show, Ascot, in September each year. A handler may qualify many times for this event and now the JHA offers a beautiful shield for the person who qualifies the most times during the year.

The semi-finals are very exciting and are often a great place to meet juniors from all over the UK. Around 400 handlers will enter, hoping to win their age group class to gain a place in the prestigious Junior Handler of the Year Finals. Instead of having just two age group classes for everyone, the handlers are divided into breed group classes and then separated into their age group classes. So, in total, there are 14 classes – two age classes (6-11 and 12-16 years) in each group, i.e. Hound, Gundog, Utility, Terrier, Toy, Working and Pastoral. This system only operates in the semi-finals. The Final is just like a normal class with 14 handlers competing.

The classes are assessed by separate judges, the majority of whom are ex-Junior Handlers and this often gives the youngsters an added incentive to perform well in this competition. To become a JHA member, it costs £2 a year and this ensures that you will be able to compete at the semi-finals, if you have won a diploma.

Junior Handler of the Year

The 14 class winners are then invited to compete in the UK Junior Handler of the Year Finals, which are held at the Metropole Hotel in Birmingham each

Marina with Kissy, and the UK Junior Handler of the Year trophies, 1998.

January (sponsored by Pedigree Petfoods). It is a very well-run event, held in conjunction with the Champion and Veteran Stakes Finals. It is also very prestigious, with nearly all the top breeders and judges in the country present. The handlers are treated to a lovely three-course meal prior to the competition but some competitors are too nervous to eat – I know I was!

The Veteran Stakes Finals are usually judged first and then it is the juniors' turn. All 14 handlers (paired next to each other in their respective groups) are introduced into the ring by the commentator. Then the judge is introduced, who puts each handler through his paces.

After all the handlers and their dogs have been seen, the judge picks the best seven, who then leave the ring to be given a different breed to handle. The handlers have already chosen the two breeds they would prefer.

The officials always use the dogs from the Veteran Stakes finals. This is often a real privilege, as most of the veterans are Champions, or even breed record holders, so you know you are handling an excellent specimen of the breed.

When I competed in my Final, I handled a Welsh Springer, Sh. Ch. Russethill Royal Salute over Nyliram who is still the breed record holder.

One by one, each of the seven finalists are introduced back into the ring with their different breed and then the judge assesses their handling skills once more.

After all the handlers and their charges have been seen, they are requested to leave the ring with those dogs and return with their original dog. The judge then chooses the winner and the runner-up, down to seventh place.

The prizes are very generous; some of the money is sponsored by Mrs Cartledge's Ryslip Kennels and also from other Championship shows. The over-all winner and runner-up, in addition to the prize money, win an all-expenses paid trip to compete at a European dog show later that year.

The Kennel Club Junior Organisation (KCJO)

The Junior Handling Association is not the only organisation to encourage youngsters into showing their dog. The Kennel Club Junior Organisation, known as the KCJO, was set up by The Kennel Club in 1985 and includes many activities, events and competitions to do with dogs, not just handling.

The KCJO has a slightly different rule, by which the members have to be aged between 8 and 18 years old. A Council, appointed by the General Committee of The Kennel Club runs the KCJO. The KCJO is separated into eight different regions with a regional organiser for each. The eight regions are:

- North West
- North East
- Midlands
- South East & East Anglia
- South & South West
- Scotland
- Wales
- Northern Ireland.

KCJO Activities

Obedience, Agility, Handling, Biathlon, Triathlon,

and Flyball are just some of the competitions that members can enter.

To become a member of the KCJO, you must pay an annual subscription of £7. This price includes free KCJO newsletters published four times a year (one for each season) and which give updates on all KCJO activities, results, pen-pal addresses, articles on doggy activities and up-and-coming events.

The yearly subscription also includes a chance to purchase Crufts main ring tickets earlier than the general public and each KCJO member gains free entry to Crufts itself. It is well worth the money to be a member of both these organisations.

KCJO Show Handler Of The Year

There is only one main Junior Handling competition which the KCJO organises and qualifying is slightly different from the JHA system.

The eight regional organisers set a date each year when the KCJO Show Handler of the Year qualifying competition will be held. These qualifying competitions are quite separate from any other shows.

The handling competition is divided into three age groups: 8-11, 12-15, and 16-17. The winners of each age group class will go on to represent their region in their class in the KCJO Show Handler of the Year competition at Crufts. The winner of each age group at Crufts then compete against each other and the judge picks an overall winner who is named KCJO Show Handler of the Year. The winning handler then represents the UK in the International Junior Handling Finals held at Crufts on the last day of the show.

CHAPTER TWO

Choosing Your Breed

If you want to become involved in Junior Handling, but are unsure about which breed of dog to choose to join you in this venture, then this chapter is designed for you, and incorporates some helpful hints. The decision you make has to be positive, as you will be loving and caring for your chosen dog for many years.

Family Dogs

Your family may already have a dog, but you may be wondering whether or not he is suitable for Junior Handling. For example, he may be a Border Collie which competes regularly in Agility competitions. Now this is a tough one, because if your Collie hasn't been properly schooled for the show ring, you are both going to be learning new skills. It is also more difficult if your dog is over two years of age, as he will have passed the stage of learning quickly and of being disciplined into new skills. Nevertheless, it is still possible to train such a dog, but only if you have the patience and the determination to succeed.

Popular Breeds

I have compiled lists of some of the most popular breeds I have seen used in Junior Handling classes over the years. Also, in order to help you to learn, and to distinguish one breed from another, they are separated into 'table dogs' and 'floor dogs'. The best way to find out about show dogs, and dog showing, is by going along to a local dog show (without your dog) and sitting, watching and observing what goes on.

Table and Floor Dogs

It is essential to know which breeds are assessed on the floor and which are assessed on the table. Part of the judging process involves the judge 'going over' a dog which is in show pose, while he is standing. The judge runs his hands over the dog to feel his conformation and to inspect his mouth and dentition. If the smallest breed in the world, the Chihuahua, were being shown on the floor, the judge would have to get down on his hands and knees to assess the dog's attributes.

That is why smaller breeds are shown on the table when they are being judged individually, hence the name 'table dogs'. Larger breeds, such as the German Shepherd Dog, the Samoyed or the Irish Wolfhound, are obviously far too big to be assessed on the table; they are a few examples of 'floor dogs'.

GUNDOG GROUP

FLOOR DOGS

English Setter
German Shorthaired Pointer (GSP)
Gordon Setter
Hungarian Vizsla
Irish Red and White Setters
Irish Setter
Pointer
Retriever (Flat Coated)
Retriever (Golden)
Retriever (Labrador)
Spaniel (English Springer)
Spaniel (Welsh Springer)
Weimaraner

TABLE DOGS

American Cocker Spaniel
Cocker Spaniel

Characteristics

Dogs in the Gundog group are mainly bred to retrieve game, sometimes from the water. Many of the breeds are cheerful, friendly and have a wonderful extrovert character. As you may already have noticed, the large majority of gundogs are 'floor' dogs and this indicates that they are too big to be assessed on the table. As most of the breeds are quite large, you need to be fairly fit when moving them for the judge.

However, a couple of the 'floor' breeds include the English Springer Spaniel and the Welsh Springer Spaniel, although their height is only 51 cm (20 in) and 46-48 cm (18-19 in) respectively. These two Springers are not quite as tall as some of the other Gundog breeds, so they would suit the slightly shorter handler.

The two types of Springer and Cocker mentioned are shown with more tension on the lead around the neck, to keep the head up. This also allows the handler to have more control of the dog.

Many of the Gundogs are excellent family dogs, including the Cocker Spaniel. The show Cocker is relatively easy to train as he thrives on human companionship. This is a great breed to handle as he is not too small to get lost around your feet, yet he is not too big. Another popular breed is the Golden

Retriever, which is larger all round but responds well to show training. Not only is the Golden one of the most popular breeds in the world, but he can be trained to perform almost anything, including being a guide dog, an explosives/drug detecting dog, an obedience expert or even an agility dog.

HOUND GROUP

FLOOR DOGS

Afghan Hound
Basset Hound
Borzoi
Deerhound
Elkhound
Greyhound
Irish Wolfhound
Rhodesian Ridgeback
Saluki

TABLE DOGS

Basenji
Beagle
Miniature Smoothhaired Dachshund
Miniature Longhaired Dachshund
Miniature Wirehaired Dachshund
Smoothhaired Dachshund
Longhaired Dachshund
Wirehaired Dachshund
Whippet

Characteristics

The Hound group comprises two types of breed – Sighthounds and Scenthounds. The difference between the two is quite obvious. The Scenthounds (i.e. Basset, Beagle, all varieties of Dachshund, Elkhound, and Rhodesian Ridgeback) are bred to hunt small animals, using their excellent sense of smell. The rest of the breeds in my list (i.e. Afghan, Whippet, Basenji, Borzoi, Deerhound, Irish Wolfhound, Saluki and Greyhound) are classed as Sighthounds, as they possess exceptional sight skills that help them hunt all sorts of prey.

The breeds in this group are all very different in character and showing style. The Irish Wolfhound is a difficult breed to handle, even for the professionals, because of its sheer size (a yard high at the shoulder makes it the tallest breed in the world). Just think what happens when you begin to move the gentle giant. A beginner, I don't care how old, would be struggling to keep up, let alone bring it to a stop!

The Afghan Hound is a wonderful, elegant breed to handle but can be a touch aloof at times. This breed can look quite spectacular standing or on the move, due to his long glossy coat and springing step. For a beginner, to have the responsibility of training, caring for and grooming the coat at least once a day is quite a task. Remember, larger dogs are more difficult to handle when moving, as they require extra control and balance from the handler.

Beagles are very similar to Cocker Spaniels, as they are both roughly the same size and need to be stacked (see Chapter 5). Although, having said that, Beagles can look great if they are trained to

TERRIER GROUP
FLOOR DOGS
Airedale Terrier
Irish Terrier
Kerry Blue Terrier
Soft-Coated Wheaten Terrier (SCWT)
Staffordshire Bull Terrier (SBT)
TABLE DOGS
Australian Terrier
Bedlington Terrier
Border Terrier
Cairn Terrier
Norfolk Terrier
Norwich Terrier
Parson Russell Terrier
Scottish Terrier
Skye Terrier
West Highland White Terrier (WHWT)
Wire Fox Terrier

free-stand. They can be moved either with a low loose lead or on a high tensioned one, running or walking. When I compete in handling classes, I tighten the lead around the dog's neck a little and this helps to keep him more alert and balanced.

Characteristics

Many of the breeds in the Terrier group are shown in exactly the same way. This excludes the SBT, Bedlington and Skye Terrier as their tails do not require to be held. The rest of the terriers require one hand firmly holding the lead up around the dogs' neck and the other hand supporting the tail. The terriers are deliberately shown with the dogs' head under control as they can be a little assertive towards other dogs. In general, all terriers are great performers who can be trained quite easily in capable hands. When shown correctly, the Junior Handler can achieve straight lines and tight turns because of the terrier's natural alertness.

The Airedale Terrier is a good sturdy breed to handle as he gets on very well with families, especially children. Even though he is the tallest of all the terriers (standing at roughly 23 inches at the shoulders) it is possible to move him easily without losing control.

The Staffordshire Bull Terrier is the only breed that I have seen not to be shown side-on when presented to the judge. He can be quite a handful as a puppy because of his naturally bold character but he gets on very well with children.

A personal favourite breed of mine is the West Highland White Terrier, not just because it is one of the most popular of the Terriers! His friendly character and perfect petite size makes him a very adaptive handling dog.

UTILITY GROUP

FLOOR DOGS

Bulldog
Chow Chow
Dalmatian
Japanese Akita
Standard Poodle

TABLE DOGS

Boston Terrier
German Spitz (Klein and Mittel)
Lhasa Apso
Miniature Schnauzer
Toy and Miniature Poodles
Shih Tzu
Tibetan Spaniel

Characteristics

The Utility Group includes many dissimilar breeds. You may notice that quite a few have countries specified in their names, hence the diversity. Many of the 'Utilities' require a tremendous amount of grooming, including the Lhasa Apso. This sturdy, characteristic breed often gets confused with the Shih Tzu and vice versa as they look quite similar.

One way to spot the difference – an adult Shih Tzu has his head hair tied back with a band, whereas an adult Lhasa Apso's head hair is left natural.

They both require daily grooming as the coats can easily become matted. One thing I must point out is that just because some breeds have long hair to cover their legs and paws, doesn't mean you don't have to place the feet. To an untrained eye, a handler may seem to have a long-coated breed with its paws in the correct position, when actually it doesn't.

In comparison, the Dalmatian, a short-coated breed, has an extrovert and active nature. It is a very tireless breed which is always shown free-standing, so requires thorough training as a puppy and hard work continually by a patient handler.

My favourite breed in this group is the majestic and powerful Japanese Akita. When handled with a firm and dominant grip, this breed can look stunning when standing and on the move. In the wrong hands, he could overcome an inexperienced Junior Handler as he can tend to be protective, but he does make a good challenge for all aspects of handling.

WORKING GROUP
FLOOR DOGS
Boxer
Bullmastiff
Dobermann
Great Dane
Newfoundland
Rottweiler
Siberian Husky

Characteristics

You will have noticed that there are no 'table dogs' listed because, yes, you guessed it, each breed in this particular group is too big to stand on a little table! Until a few years ago the Working group contained many more breeds but it was then decided that there were too many breeds in this group. The Kennel Club split the Working group into two groups, Pastoral and the Working group.

The Doberman and Rottweiler both have a very similar handling style. They naturally freestand with the owner standing directly in front with discreet titbits. Some Junior Handlers as well as adults in breed showing, tend to bait the Dobermann with titbits in their right hand and kneel down beside the dog.

The Boxer has a strong build and he uses this power to stride nobly around the ring. The handler has to make sure that the Boxer moves in a straight line, as the powerful hindquarters can tend to push this breed off balance more than other breeds. This breed is mostly baited or strung up with a shorter lead; the tail needs to be pushed up as well.

PASTORAL GROUP

FLOOR DOGS

Bearded Collie
Belgian Shepherd Dog (Tervueren)
Border Collie
German Shepherd Dog
Old English Sheepdog
Rough Collie
Samoyed

TABLE DOGS

Hugarian Puli
Shetland Sheepdog
Welsh Corgi (Pembroke and Cardigan)

Characteristics

Having only just handled a Shetland Sheepdog for the first time last year, with whom I was delighted to win my first BIS at an Open show, I found that they are not as timid as you might think. A little reserved at first, they are attentive and inquisitive about what you might have in your pocket. This is an attractive looking dog that moves neatly round the ring and one which you can quickly form a rapport with.

Marina with a Bearded Collie, a member of the Pastoral group.

A Bearded Collie is an ideal size for someone of my height (5ft 2ins). It is a very glamorous looking breed when in full coat and can move around the ring smoothly with tremendous speed. In profile, the handler may hold the head with the right hand or string the dog's head up using some tension on the lead. A breed suited to anyone who doesn't want to fuss about with a tail, just using combs to groom the coat.

TOY GROUP
TABLE DOGS
Bichon Frise
Cavalier King Charles Spaniel (C.K.C.S)
Chihuahua
Chinese Crested Dog
Italian Greyhound
Maltese
Papillon
Pomeranian
Yorkshire Terrier

Characteristics

The Toy group represents a classification of breeds that are small – just as the name suggests! The breeds in this group are ideal for anyone that would prefer a different style of handling, as some are freestood (e.g the C.K.C.S, Chinese Crested, Papillon and Pomeranian) because of their size.

It is essential, when training with a small breed, to build up a rapport by playing and generally having fun. The dog should be watching and listening to you at all times. These small breeds move at a quicker pace than you would think!

A popular handling breed from this group is the Bichon Frise which is a compact and friendly dog for the younger handler. This breed is of moderate weight to lift onto the table, but requires thorough and precise grooming for the show ring.

The Papillon is a great breed to handle as it simply glides round the ring when moving and seems to enjoy every minute of the show ring. Again, grooming is required, but only before going into the ring. Some handlers like to take a little comb in their pocket to tidy any loose or straggly hairs.

CHAPTER THREE

Getting Started

To be honest, there is no wrong way to begin handling, but there are some things you can do to make the process a little easier. Buy a specialist book about your breed. It is very important to know what the dogs were bred for. Was it for hunting, or retrieving, or for going to ground? You also need to know which Group the breed is in and how the dog should be presented. Should he be free-standing or stacked? These terms will be explained later.

Breed books also provide you with useful information about such matters as the Breed Standards, general care, health and breeding. They often do have a small section on showing but it is very basic and does not go into enough detail about the appropriate aspects of handling.

Ring-craft Classes

The next step is to find the nearest ring-craft training classes and it is definitely an advantage if there is a Junior Handling expert there, or at least someone who knows the show handling procedures.

Fortunately, Junior Handling is being taken more and more seriously, so now even the adults are hoping to get a few helpful hints. Make sure that you are going to a ring-craft class and not one for Agility or Obedience, because these classes are completely different.

A ring-craft class is normally organised by a Dog Club or Society on a weekday evening, in a hall of some kind, and some are bigger than others. If you are training a very large breed, it is sometimes well worth travelling that bit further to a bigger venue. This type of dog-related class is designed to socialise and train you and your dog into the world of breed showing. Do not get confused; remember that the judge in breed showing is specifically judging your dog, whereas in Junior Handling the judge is judging the handler.

In addition to the normal routine training, the club or society may hold specialist talks from accredited dog trainers or even have fun party nights to increase the already prominent enthusiasm from dog showers. It is very noticeable that dog showing becomes a large part of your own social life. Once you join training classes, you meet many wonderful people then head off to your first show and you will be astounded with the immediate enthusiasm from everyone all around.

The Initial Visit

I was very lucky because when I first became interested in showing, my mother had already competed at many shows. She had absorbed a lot of knowledge and experience that she then could pass on to me.

If you are going to training classes for the very first time, initially visit without your dog so that you can familiarise and socialise yourself with other people and their dogs. You can introduce yourself to the trainers there and they will gladly give you advice and perhaps even certain rules of their club. For example, they may have a separate time in the evening, or a separate night, when puppies can be trained. The trainers at your ring craft classes will point you in the right direction, especially if you are a beginner. You may want to attend a few weekly classes before you take your dog but, when you do, it is very important to keep him under control at all times.

Your Learning Dog

You may also be lucky enough to practise with a good tempered and well-behaved show dog. This will help you to gain confidence while you are still learning the basics. Do not start with a puppy, because they are unpredictable and are liable to throw you off balance, plus the puppy is learning too. Not a good combination!

Absorbing Atmosphere

It will also help a great deal if you take a few minutes to sit and absorb the atmosphere in the hall. You can learn quite a lot of the basics by watching what everyone else is doing but remember, they may be learning as well. You may notice that all the handlers have the lead in the left hand and not in both hands. This not only gives you more balance but also keeps the dog stable as you are holding the lead right above the dog's body and not to his side.

Using Treats

Once you feel comfortable enough to take your own dog along to the training classes, there are a couple of things you can do which could save a lot of bother. Take a few dog biscuits, just in case your dog gets frightened and manages to slip out of his collar, and then you can use the titbits to (hopefully) get him back.

Such treats are also useful when showing, because it can often relax the dog if he is chewing on some biscuits while strange people are 'going over' him.

'Going Over'

This term is used to describe the process whereby the judge uses his hands to feel the dog's structure (which he may not be able to do by just looking) and proceeds quietly from the dog's head to the rear end.

A bum-bag is a useful way to keep hold of your titbits when at training classes. Personally, when competing, I think it looks tidier without.

Show Leads

You must use the correct show lead, even at training classes. If your dog has got his normal walking collar and lead on, he will behave as if he is going for a walk.

Your dog must learn that, when he is wearing his show lead, he should associate it with show training (see Chapter 4 on more about the correct lead type to use for your breed).

Training Gear

At training classes, you don't have to dress up formally as you are not being judged, but practising. So wear a simple t-shirt, comfortable trousers and trainers.

Training Manners

Do not let your dog sniff at other dogs' behinds. This is not only incredibly annoying for the other dog's handler but also for the dog, as most dogs are very protective about their rear end. Remember also to keep your dog on a short lead and do not let him be noisy.

Training Movements

If the hall is big enough, you may all be told to move your dogs around in a circle. The trainers will then assess each dog, one by one, as happens at a normal show, but they will be giving you help and advice along the way to achieve a better performance, both for you and your dog. The trainer will most probably get you to do a triangle and an up-and-down, as these are the easiest patterns to start with. Find out how to achieve these patterns in Chapter 7.

Types of Show

- Championship
- Open
- Limited
- Exemption.

There are four types of dog shows that you can enter with a KC registered dog, which vary according to the number of exhibits and the size of the venue, with the Exemption show being the smallest and the Championship show the largest. Junior Handling classes are scheduled mostly at Exemption, Open and Championship level.

Championship Shows

There are 25 General (all breeds) Championship shows a year and they can be held over two, three or four days. This is because the number of entries (dogs) is so high – between 6,000 and 20,000. The 25 shows are spread throughout the country, incorporating Northern Ireland, Scotland, England and Wales (see p.40).

At the Championship shows, the quality of the Junior Handling classes is usually quite high. Juniors from all over the country compete for a place in the line-up from 1st to 5th. Many of these shows offer the JHA qualifiers for Richmond. The entries reflect this, as each handling class can range from 15-60 but remember these are the entries; not all the handlers will necessarily turn up on the day.

The KCJO also schedule their own handling classes at some of the Championship shows as well as the JHA classes. Do not get confused; if you

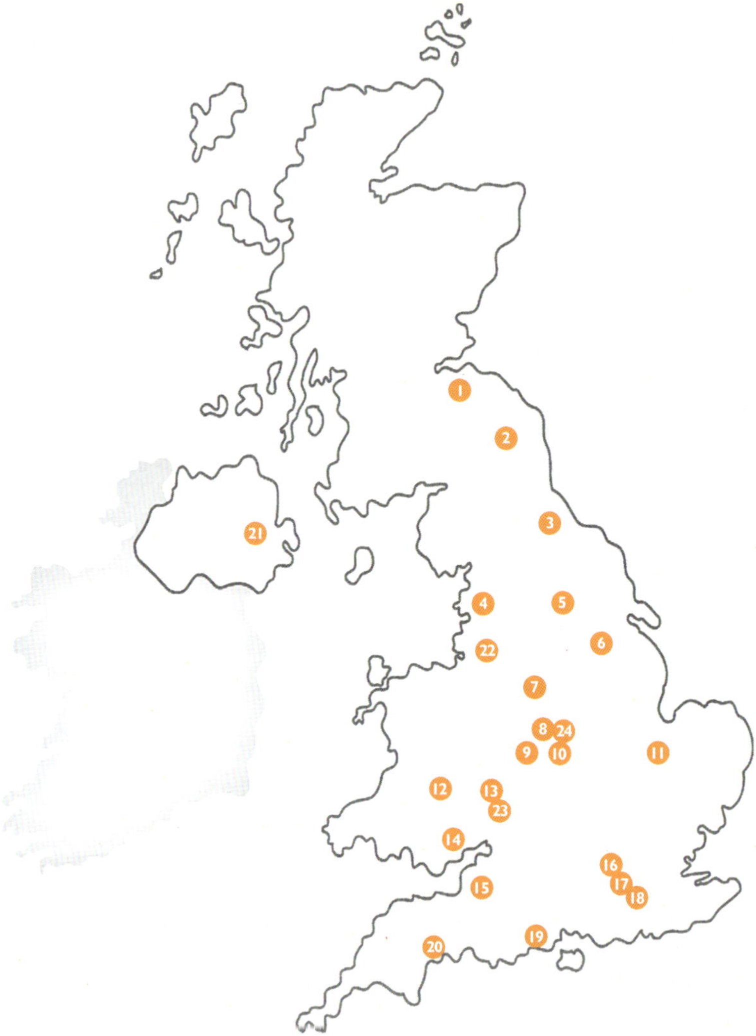

1 Scottish Kennel Club (2 held per year)
2 Border Union
3 Darlington
4 Blackpool
5 Leeds
6 Driffield
7 Midland Counties
8 L.K.A.
9 Crufts
10 Birmingham National
11 East of England
12 Welsh K.C.
13 Three Counties
14 South Wales
15 Bath
16 Windsor
17 Richmond
18 Southern Counties
19 Bournemouth
20 Paignton
21 Belfast
22 Manchester
23 W. E. L. K. S.
24 City of Birmingham

are a member of both clubs, you can enter both. This can make for an interesting day, as each class has a different judge. However, the KCJO schedules four classes (8-11 years, 12-15 years, 16-17 years and 18 years) instead of the JHA's two (6-11 years and 12-16 years). Remember that the winner of each KCJO class at a Championship show does not qualify for the KCJO Show Handler of the Year.

Open Shows

Open shows, in my opinion, are just as much fun because there are many more juniors you recognise from your local area and it is easier to win a placing, due to the lower entries. However, the Junior Handling classes nowadays are often well filled due to prizes such as JHA qualifiers, trophies and chocolate being on offer. The latter appeals to me!

I suggest that, if you are competing for your very first time, it is better to enter at an Open show; don't suddenly jump in at the big Championship show, where you are inexperienced and likely to get much more nervous.

At Championship shows, it is possible to qualify your dog for Crufts in the breed classes but at Open shows you can't; although you can qualify at Open shows if you win a Best in Show (BIS), a Reserve Best in Show (RBIS) or a Best Puppy in Show (BPIS) award.

Entry Requirements

At nearly all Championship and Open shows it is a requirement to enter yourself and your dog for the show prior to the closing date. Remember that you may not take any dog into any type of dog show unless the dog is Kennel Club registered and has been entered beforehand.

It is a Kennel Club rule that all Junior Handlers must have their dog entered in another breed class at the show. This means that you can borrow other people's dogs for use in the Junior Handling classes, as long as they are entered in another class at the same show.

Advance Entries

On most entry forms there is a space where you write your name and age. You must complete the rest of the entry form correctly and clearly, as it will then be easier for the show secretary and printers to process. Whoever owns your dog **must** sign the form in the bottom left-hand corner.

When sending an entry away, always enclose a SAE or a postcard with the name of the show at the top and the words 'Your entry has been received and entered' underneath. Then, leave a place for the secretary to date and sign. This is just for personal peace of mind so that you know the secretary has definitely received your entry. Also complete a form of certified post proof of posting, e.g. Recorded Delivery, Special Delivery, Registered Post, Post Office Certificate (obtained from the Post Office), as this is the only evidence the Kennel Club will accept as proof of entry if anything were to go missing. NB. The K.C. accept original copies only.

A sample entry form can be seen on page 188 (appendix).

'On The Day' Entries

Some Open shows and all Exemption shows don't require the Junior Handler to enter beforehand. They call it 'enter on the day' and that's exactly what you do! The average cost to enter a handling class at an Exemption or Open show is about 75p. At Championship Shows, the cost to enter is approximately £3. Do remember that the dog you handle in the Junior Handling classes must be entered in the show.

The Handler: **Helena Hutchings**

Helena, from south-east England, has been one of the most prolific winners as a Junior Handler in the UK but has just come to the end of that particular phase in her life. She continues her interest in dog shows by competing in breed showing and by judging Junior Handling and breeds in the Pastoral Group. She practises regularly by attending three ring craft classes. She has already started to show other people's dogs and she hopes that this will help her to become a professional handler.

She first became interested in dog showing when she was eight years old, after she and her mother bought two puppies and took them to the local pet obedience class. The trainer there suggested they should try showing them. When only one of the puppies would co-operate, Helena decided to learn how to handle – and then trained the pup! Her curiosity grew when she was encouraged to show not only in the breed classes but also to become involved in Junior Handling.

Helena has been showing her Belgian Shepherd Dog since she was eight years old.

The Group: **Pastoral**

This Group encompasses all the herding breeds such as the Border Collie and the Shetland Sheepdog.

The Breed: **Belgian Shepherd Dog (Tervueren)**

Showing style: ***Floor dog***
Helena is well known for showing her Tervueren, which requires regular brushing. For the show ring, Belgian Shepherd Dogs should have their legs and feet trimmed to ensure neat and tidy paws. This is a free-standing breed, shown four-square and baited from the front to gain the typical Belgian expression. When competing in the breed classes, some owners show the dog 'head-on' to the judge, as this is the Continental style. However, for Junior Handling competitions, the dog should be shown side-on. When moving this breed in the pattern work, they need to be shown at a moderate to fast pace, on a slack lead. The ears should be erect at all times, so the dog requires to be baited. The tail should never be carried above the dog's top line when moving.

Other Favourites

Helena has handled many other breeds in Junior Handling classes including the Belgian Shepherd Dog (Groenendael), Border Collies, Giant Schnauzers, Whippets, Cairn Terriers, Bearded Collies, Bichon Frisé and Weimaraners. She says that her favourite three breeds, apart from the dogs she either owns or lives with, are the Bichon, the Weimaraner and the Russian Black Terrier. These particularly appeal because they require a totally different showing style from her normal Belgian and they are really flashy.

Dress Sense

When she competes in competition, Helena wears a royal blue coloured jacket with a white, high-necked top underneath. On the lower half, she wears either white trousers or a royal blue knee-length skirt. On her feet she wears white soft lace-up shoes.

Achievements

Helena has competed well over the years, bringing many titles home with her from the UK and Europe. These include the Pedigree Chum Junior Handler of

Helena has won many titles in JH from the UK and Europe.

the Year Winner 1996, Runner-up Pedigree Chum Junior Handler of the year 1997 and 1999, KCJO Show Handler of the Year Winner 1997, 1998 and 1999, and Runner-up International Junior Handler of the Year 1997, 1998 and 1999. In 2001 she represented Monaco at the International Handler of the Year Final.

Memorable Moments

Her most memorable occasion was winning her first Challenge Certificate (CC) with her first show dog, named Ria, at Richmond Championship Show. On that day she had already won through to the UK Junior Handler of the Year finals so, when she was awarded the CC, she felt she had never been so happy.

The most unusual incident has to be when she was at a show in Monte Carlo. She was asked to handle a Corralien Bear Dog in the class and he just would not co-operate, however hard she tried. Then the judge came over to the dog and just whispered in his ear. After that, the Corralien behaved as if he was a Crufts Best In Show Winner!

Top Tip

Helena loves the satisfaction which comes from competing and also from winning. She cherishes working with her dogs and meeting new people along the way. Her helpful tip is to remember to enjoy it all. She says: "make sure you have fun time with your dog and, if you win, it is a bonus."

Finding Shows

Most Championship shows advertise in the weekly dog press, either *Dog World* or *Our Dogs*, two months before the actual date of the show. There is normally an address and/or phone number to contact to receive a schedule. The advertisement will also provide the closing date by which you must have sent off your entry form. This is very important, as many shows do not accept any entry forms after this date. Make sure your entry form is sent at least a week before the closing date to avoid problems such as a postal strike or illness. You can also pick up many schedules from attending your local ring-craft class, or Open and Championship shows.

Show Checklist

- Buy *Dog World* or *Our Dogs* from newsagent
- Phone for a schedule
- Receive schedule with entry form
- Fill in and send away entry form, SAE and certified post certificate.
- Receive confirmation of entry
- File SAE/and post certificate with schedule
- Attend show.

CHAPTER FOUR

Presentation

The presentation of the Junior Handler has improved greatly over the years. However, it does require some forethought, as the wrong presentation can, on occasions, prevent the judge from placing you first, even if you have performed a near perfect round.

The Handler

The presentation of the handler is basically about what you wear when you compete in the ring. You might think slipping on a comfortable pair of tracksuit bottoms, a T-shirt and trainers would be acceptable, but you're wrong. If you wore that, you wouldn't get very far but you would blend in really well with the Agility competitors! In Junior Handling, it is essential to wear appropriate clothing which complements the dog. This includes thinking about material, shape, colour and fit.

Girls

Nowadays, the girls tend to wear a trouser-suit of matching colours with a separate coloured top/blouse underneath the jacket. When I first began showing, I wore a waistcoat with a blouse underneath. That is quite acceptable but, unfortunately, my lower half wasn't so well dressed. I wore a long green skirt that draped over my Beagle's head (below). In hindsight this was a bad mistake.

Long flowing skirts are never a good idea because they get in the way of the dog and distract the judge's eye. Today, you don't often see girls wearing skirts; this is because a lot of leaning over and/or

Long flowing skirts (left) are not advisable.

The colour of your outfit should be dictated by your dog. A bright, contrasting pink jacket helps the handler stand out much easier than a grey one.

running is required, especially when showing a large breed.

Wearing a knee-length skirt can look very smart and feminine but only if you are showing a breed that is just required to freestand. Remember to wear tights (either see-through or opaque) as the weather can turn very chilly within a matter of seconds in some places. I have seen a young handler wearing a short-cropped top with her neat trousers but, of course, this was not suitable. Skimpy tops are for beach use, not for the show ring.

Boys

The boys sport either a suit or, sometimes, a waistcoat and smart trousers. I must emphasise that when I am referring to trousers, I don't mean jeans. Jeans look as if you haven't bothered to dress properly at all, although, when I judged at a show in Scotland a few years ago, I reluctantly put the

Junior handlers must present themselves as well as their dogs, so a smart appearance is essential.

12-16 years winner, who wore jeans, Best Junior Handler. After the competition, I advised the handler not to wear jeans again and this I also emphasised in the critique. This particular handler was placed first and Best Handler overall because of the excellent handling skills demonstrated, but not all judges would have necessarily placed that handler first.

If you are wearing a tie, ensure it is tucked away inside your jacket or use a simple safety pin to pin it to your shirt. A flapping tie in the wind could attract your dog's attention, even if you are standing in show pose.

Materials

When choosing your clothing, remember to think about the type of material used. Preferably you want one that does not pick up dog hairs and dirt too easily. Materials such as velvet, silk or any other delicate, fine or feathery material are just not practical for dog handling, let alone affordable!

A good tip for keeping your neat suit flat and crease-free before going into the ring is to take a hanger and zip-up cover with you to the show. Many handlers carry their attire like this when travelling to a show and don't actually get changed into their 'posh' gear until they arrive.

Colour

The colour of your outfit is probably the most important aspect of the dress code. It is essential that you choose a colour that complements the coat colour of your dog. By this, I mean picking a colour that is either the opposite of your dog's coat colour or a colour which highlights the dog's outline. For example, a Dobermann (usually black and tan) would stand out against a pair of white trousers; or a Maltese (pure white) would look lovely against black material.

When showing a table dog, remember that your upper half is in the spotlight, and so dress accordingly.

I wear black trousers when I show my Beagles because they happen to be mostly white with some tan and a touch of black. I used to show a dark tri-beagle puppy, and she was mostly black with tan so I took my white trousers and changed into them when I showed her.

If you have a breed that has either two or more colours, choose contrasting colours. Remember that your upper half needs to be considered as well when deciding on colours. If the judge is assessing a 'table' dog, the handler's upper body would be in the background, as it is at the same height as the dog.

My usual attire at a show consists of black trousers, with a black top underneath a coral-coloured jacket. I have rarely needed to change from what I wear, as the colours go with most breeds that I have shown.

Footwear

Footwear is also very important as it completes the overall impression of a neat and tidy handler. Many handlers, both boys and girls, still seem to think trainers are okay to wear. I know it is important to be comfortable when handling, but there are other types of cosy, flat shoes which you can wear without them having designer labels tacked on the sides.

I suggest either court shoes, deck shoes or plimsolls

for girls; try to stick to lower heels for better balance when moving your dog. I wear black court shoes that have a slight heel because I'm quite short and I try to portray myself as being a little taller.

For boys, I would suggest any type of shoe that falls into these categories: lightweight, dark grey/black, no heel (that is if any of you do wear heels!), good grip and practical.

Pockets

If you have a breed that requires titbits during your round, you will obviously need somewhere to put them. I recommend making sure you have pockets in your jacket or waistcoat, or using a bum bag, provided it is not too big. Some exhibitors who show toy breeds have small shoulder bags to contain their treats. You may also need a place to put brushes or combs for grooming your dog while in the ring, so ensure that your pockets are large enough.

Weather Essentials

You also have to remember that the weather can change very quickly, so you always have to be prepared to adapt to the conditions. I never go to any show without wellington boots, an umbrella and a waterproof coat. They are vital for any regular competitor because you are then completely equipped for any type of weather condition. On this note, you may even have to think about buying specialist boots or shoes for your dog. Some long-coated breeds, such as the Samoyed or the Afghan Hound, are often seen at the shows with doggy-designed shoes on to protect the long fur around their paws and keep it clean and tidy, especially if it is wet under foot.

Hair

If your striking outfit complements the dog's colour perfectly, you don't want your hair to be either in the way or flapping about distracting the judge. Obviously most boys do not have to make as much effort as the girls, but a lick of gel would do fine to keep any straggling hairs back.

If you have long hair (shoulder-length and below) the best way is to scoop it up into a bun and wrap round either a matching colour scrunchie or some other hair accessory that matches your outfit. This may well impress the judge because you have made that extra effort to look your best.

I always put my hair up in a bun and clip back any loose hairs with hair grips. If I am competing at a prestigious event I would put a couple of artificial pink flowers in the bun to look extra groomed. It is also handy if you use a hair net, as you will find that bits of hair will work themselves out of the bun. Take plenty of clips, hairspray and spare hair bands to the show, especially if you are outdoors, as it can get very windy.

Accessories

It is very easy to go over the top with accessories such as watches and jewellery. I have judged handlers who are wearing far too many rings; it looks so untidy. Think very basic; even watches can be taken off when in the ring. Don't wear any necklaces or bracelets; it is just not necessary and it will distract the judge's eye from the dog. For prestigious events, I wear small stud earrings to look slightly more glamorous.

Ring Card Holders

When you go into the ring, the steward will give you your ring number (which will also be in the catalogue). This number has to be displayed at all times when in the ring. It is important because it allows spectators and exhibitors to find out who you are (by looking your number up in the catalogue), but more importantly, not the judge. Exhibitor's names are not passed to the judge beforehand in order to ensure that the individual performances on the day are judged impartially.

The most common way to show your number is to pin a dog clip on to somewhere convenient on your outfit. These clips are designed to hold the cards and there are many different styles on offer. If you want to be extra smart and tidy, then you can also buy ring cardholders for your arm. They are plastic, wrap around the top of your arm and are joined by either Velcro or buttons. Here, the card number slots into the clear plastic. Or a cheap and easy way is to use an elastic band to wrap the card around your arm.

Many handlers like to pin badges onto their show jacket. This is acceptable but try to limit the number of clips you pin on to your jacket or waistcoat, as it can look very fussy. I only wear two or three clips; one for my ring card and the others are my handling and membership badges.

The Dog

This involves tasks like bathing, grooming and also using the correct colour and lead type for your breed.

The Handler: **Kelly McWilliams**

Kelly, from Fife in Scotland, caught the showing bug at a young age because most of her family either owned or showed dogs. At the age of seven she made a few hesitant steps into the ring herself and soon began showing her family's Dobermann. She then progressed to other breeds. She wants to continue her doggy interest after Junior Handling by judging and continuing in breed showing.

The Group: **Working Group**

This includes a multitude of breeds such as guard dogs, for example Boxers and Rottweilers, and all-purpose breeds including German Shepherd Dogs.

The Breed: **Dobermann**

Showing style: ***Floor dog***

A Dobermann can be presented to the judge either free-standing or stacked, depending on the handler's preference. Kelly prefers to free-stand her dogs, which takes a lot of practice to get it right. The breed is moved at a steady pace to show the good reach of the forequarters and the drive in the hindquarters, although the handler has to jog slightly to keep up. To get the Dobermann's short coat smooth and close-lying, a little grooming using a horse brush and then a velvet cloth is required before any show. It is also essential to file the dog's nails regularly, to keep them short and neat.

Kelly, with Mica, a Dobermann.

Other Favourites

Kelly has shown a total of eight different breeds in competition: The Boxer, the Newfoundland, a Miniature Schnauzer, a Rottweiler, a German Shorthaired Pointer (GSP), a German Wirehaired Pointer, an English Springer Spaniel and the Bedlington Terrier. Kelly feels she has been lucky to have shown some of her favourite breeds, particularly Boxers,

Kelly prefers to free-stand her dogs.

because of their cheeky faces, and the Miniature Schnauzers, with their little grand-dad faces and feisty characters. She also loves Miniature Poodles and their showiness and motoring movement.

Dress Sense

When showing a Dobermann, Kelly wears a white top, white trousers and white trainers with a bright green suit jacket on top, which brings out the dark outline of the dog.

Achievements

Kelly has acquired many Best Junior Handler awards and many placings in Junior Handling competitions.

Her best achievements were being a Pedigree Chum Junior Handler of the Year finalist twice and coming fifth in the final the second time round. She has also been a KCJO Show Handler of the Year finalist twice and was placed second and third in each final.

Memorable Moments

Her most memorable occasion was when she was nine years old and placed first at the Richmond semi-finals. She was the only Scottish Junior Handler competing on that day and it was her first time competing in the semi-finals.

The funniest thing she has seen in the ring was when a young handler was showing the family dog. The dog was more interested in seeking out his true handler and, when he did, he pulled the girl out of the ring with him!

She regularly attends ringcraft classes to practise with her dogs.

Top Tip

Kelly enjoys the pattern work of Junior Handling more than breed classes as this is when she is being judged, not the dog. Most of all she loves the fact that she has made so many friends over the years. But, together with so many other junior handlers, she hates the travelling.

Her top tip is to listen to fellow handlers and not to be scared to ask for advice.

Grooming

Accomplished handlers always do the grooming and bathing themselves. Many a time I have seen a parent brushing the dog and clipping the nails at the show when the handler is sitting around doing nothing. I know the judge is not observing this, but the handler should be caring for the dog, or at least helping out.

Certain breeds require a lot of thorough grooming and clipping; ideally this should be done the night before. I always bath my dogs the night before a show, using dog shampoo and making sure I rinse all the shampoo out. This is important because if any shampoo is left in the coat, it will be itchy and sore for the dog. However, in some breeds it is not recommended to bath the dog the night before, as the coat needs time to settle.

Straight after the bath when the nails are soft, my Mum holds each dog in turn, so I can clip the nails and trim the fur under the paws. The teeth are also brushed with a small dog toothbrush and toothpaste. Any stubborn tartar can be scraped off but be careful of the gums. I wouldn't recommend younger children scraping or brushing the teeth; it is best to leave this to the adults.

Leads

It is important to have a proper show lead for

Correct ways of holding a show lead

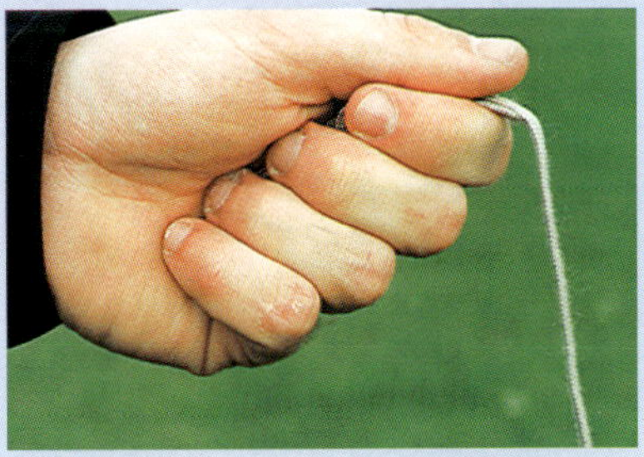

handling in the ring because, if you use the dog's normal collar and lead, he will think he is going for a walk and behave accordingly. The show lead provides extra control when standing and moving your dog. Also, using a dog's ordinary lead and collar is too heavy and distracting and, with most breeds, affects the lie of the coat.

There are several kinds of leads you can use, and in different ways. The most common type is the slip chain with a nylon lead attached to it. This lead comes in all sorts of sizes and it is important to get the right size for your breed. The slip chain can be bought in a bronze, silver or gold coating. The

Incorrect lead presentation: the dog's long coat is tangled in the lead.

Perfect presentaion – from both the dog and the handler.

nylon attachment can come in many different colours, thickness and lengths. Try to match the colour of your lead to your outfit, as this may be noted by the judge.

There is a correct way of putting on a slip chain, even though some experienced handlers still don't

Putting on a slip chain

1

2

3

4

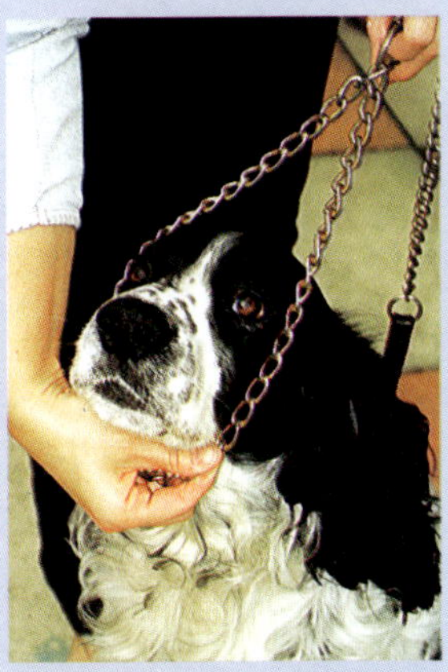

realise it! Pull part of the chain through the ring to make a large space and then put the chain over the dog's head with the other ring to the left (when you are standing in front of the dog). Try practising this by using your left hand as the dog's head and neck.

Another popular type of lead is the all-in-one nylon show lead. Smaller breeds with long coats tend to use this type, as it doesn't get caught up with the long hair, unlike the chain. Nearly all the breeds in the terrier group use the all-in-one as it offers the best control. Again, this show lead comes in many different colours; try and match it with your dress code.

Presentation Checklist

- Choose clothing materials that are practical and affordable.
- Go for colours that complement your dog.
- Footwear should be comfortable and smart.
- When packing clothes be prepared for adverse weather.
- Always keep hair tidy and out of the way.
- Practise putting on a slip chain.
- Never wear jeans, T-shirts or skimpy tops.
- Never wear trainers or high-heeled shoes.
- Do not wear too many accessories such as badges or jewellery.

CHAPTER FIVE

The Show Pose

The show pose is when the handler attempts to stand the dog in his most natural state for the breed, while ensuring that the dog's best points are highlighted, and his faults are hidden. The show pose is used in the line up, when all the handlers and their dogs are positioned in a straight line along the edge of the ring, and also when the judge assesses each dog individually.

There are a number of points to learn and to understand as you practise the show pose, as nearly every breed has its own unique style.

Stacking

Some handlers have to show their dogs with their right hand holding the dog's head and the left hand holding the tail. This is called stacking.

The only time you need to show the opposite way (dog's head in left hand and tail in right) is if the judge asks you to, or if the ground is sloping downwards from left to right. If you left the dog set up sloping downwards, its top-line would be affected, whereas if you turned the dog around, so it is facing upwards, the top line will be less unnatural.

Example of breeds that can be stacked are:

- Nearly all Gundog breeds
- Poodles
- Basset Hounds
- Beagles
- Bloodhounds
- Boxers

A 'stacked' Beagle having his head and tail supported by his handler.

Teaching Tips

When stacking your dog, you should be able to notice whether your dog is 'rocking', as this can spoil the dog's topline (the line from the withers to the rump). You can spot a dog rocking if you look

TEACHING TIPS

This Afghan is 'rocking': his front legs are not vertical to the ground, resulting in an imperfect topline and overall shape.

at him from the side, observing the dog's outline, and see the front legs leaning back, which results in the back dipping in the middle. Personally, I feel that handling a breed that requires to be stacked takes more hard work than free-standing.

Free-standing

This means that the handler baits the dog by standing in front of him. The handler may position the feet in place but is then required to return to the front to continue attracting the dog's attention. The handler has to think about feet positioning,

A free-standing Japanese Akita, presented on a taut lead.

holding the tail correctly, lead presentation and perhaps even grooming during the routine.

The Taut Lead

When free-standing a dog, the lead can be held up behind the ears with just enough tension to keep control. Sometimes the lead may be lowered to suit the individual breed. Most of the breeds in the Terrier Group are shown free-standing, with the lead taut up behind the ears, as their naturally feisty characters keep the short tails up.

Examples of breeds that can be shown with the lead held up behind the ears are:

- Bichon Frisé
- Cairn Terriers

- Great Danes
- Greyhounds
- Japanese Akita
- Salukis
- Shih Tzu
- St Bernards
- West Highland White Terriers
- Whippets
- Wire Fox Terriers

Ground To Table Differences

If a breed such as the Norfolk Terrier free-stands on the ground, he does not necessarily free-stand when on the table. The handler has to adopt a different 'stacked' style so the dog doesn't jump or fall off the table. The handler's right hand would have to hold the lead taut up behind the ears and then, if required, use the left hand to push the tail up into position.

Nearly all the toy breeds are free-stood, due to their size and shape. The handler needs to excel in attracting the dog's attention quietly but effectively. This is where a lot of dedicated practice at home can really shine through, as a rapport will soon be achieved. A lot of other breeds do not require the tail to be held, so then the handler can concentrate on head control and positioning the feet.

The Papillon is shown free-standing naturally.

Natural Free-standing

Some breeds are shown free-standing naturally, which is when the handler lets the dog pose correctly by himself. A few examples of dogs that can be shown in this way are:

- Border Collies
- Cavalier King Charles Spaniels
- Dalmatians
- Labrador Retrievers
- Papillons
- Pomeranians
- Rottweilers

- Rough Collies
- Samoyeds

Teaching Tips

Teach your dog to stand for you by first standing in front of the dog and making him stand for a couple of seconds; then praise or give him a small titbit. Then slowly build up the amount of time he free-stands, remembering to praise your dog's efforts. The next step is to teach the dog to stand while you walk around the back of him. Hopefully your dog should have understood by now what you are trying to achieve. It will get easier the more you practise. The trick when teaching your dog to stand is to build up the time slowly; otherwise he could easily break into bad habits.

When training, hold the lead in your left hand for control and use bait/signals with your right hand. Use your voice quietly at all times because your dog will have to concentrate more to hear you.

Shadowing

It is important when presenting your dog to the judge that you shadow the judge's movement quietly and smoothly. For example, if the judge moves round to assess the back legs, calmly move

SHADOWING

Shadowing is an important technique that allows the judge to assess the dog without the handler getting in the way.

around to the front of the dog, keeping his attention, using verbal or signal encouragement.

Then, if the judge moves away to look at the dog in profile, you can move back into your original position, stabilising your dog's pose. Handlers who have not practised this technique will be quite obvious to the judge, who will most probably penalise as necessary.

The Set Up For Stacked Breeds

When setting up your dog, start by moving his front legs into position by gripping the forearm and then placing the feet into the correct position. Never rush at this point as it conveys to the judge that you are nervous, which you might not be!

I always position the left foreleg first with my left hand whilst holding the lead in my right. Then I change hands and position the right foreleg. Don't forget to make sure both feet are level. The next step is to place the hind legs. You can achieve this by changing hands again and positioning the dog's hind left leg, then the right. Once again, remember to check that your dog is standing four-square.

In a stacked breed, the dog's legs should carefully be placed in correct position.

Your smooth actions will also help your dog to relax and be at ease with his surroundings. Do not let go of your dog's head while you are placing the feet, as then the dog is free to move. Do not ever kick or knee your dog into position. I have seen this happen a few times before and it is absolutely unnecessary. This unacceptable behaviour towards the dog shows that the handler is not kind and is not enjoying the competition. You should handle your dog carefully at all times, for the dog's own welfare – not just because the judge is watching you!

Another important point worth remembering is to make sure your lead is neat and tidy at all times. If you are holding your dog's head with your right hand, then you have two options about where to put your lead. You can either roll the excess lead up in your right hand whilst holding the dog's head or you can lay the lead around the dog's chest, placed on the withers.

If you place the lead around the dog's neck in between the head and the neck, this spoils the dog's outline. Remember one of the main concepts in Junior Handling is to try to get the best out of your dog. If your breed doesn't require the head to be held, then just keep the lead taught up behind the ears as again it can spoil the outline if the lead has not been correctly positioned.

Setting up the stacked dog requires placing the legs in their correct position.

When stacking, the excess lead should be held in the hand, neatly out of the way.

The Individual Pose

Floor Dogs

If your dog is a large breed and requires to be set up on the floor, position him about one metre (3.3 feet) in front of the table. If the table is at an angle, set your dog up parallel to the nearest ring side.

A trailing lead detracts attention away from the judge, and will incur a penalty.

Here, the lead is correctly coiled up in the hand, neatly out of sight.

Don't forget to leave enough space around you and your dog, so you can walk around him if necessary. Also, don't crowd your dog by being too near his body. The judge cannot see the correct outline if you are leaning over the dog.

Table Dogs

When you pick your dog up and put him onto the table, the judge may be watching, so always raise the dog carefully. Once your dog is on the table, position him more to the right of the table and then to the front because then he is easier for the judge to assess than if he was placed in the centre of the table. If the table has a very small mat that doesn't quite reach both front and back paws, I suggest putting the mat further back so that the back paws cannot slip. Remember to show 'right to left', unless the table is a long wooden one and the mat has been placed to the far left.

The Judge's Individual Assessment

For both individual table or floor dog poses, the judge will watch you for a moment from side view and then walk around to face the front of your dog. There is no need to move or change your position at this point. Make sure you are reassuring and

Talking to the dog will help to keep him focused on you.

encouraging your dog by using voice control. The judge, more than likely, will move closer to the dog's head and ask you the dog's age. Just answer simply and do not carry the conversation on.

The Mouth

The judge will then most likely ask you to show him the dog's teeth, which is also known as the dog's bite. There has always been a mixture of opinion about the difference. When I was competing, I went under two judges who penalised me for showing all the teeth when I was asked to show the bite. Yet many judges argue that the teeth and the bite mean the same thing. This yet has to be clarified. The bite can be defined as 'the relative position of the upper and lower teeth when the mouth is closed'.
There are four different types of bite:

- Scissor bite
- Level bite
- Undershot
- Overshot

Scissor Bite

Most breeds have a scissor bite which means that the upper set of teeth closely overlaps the lower set of teeth. Some examples of breeds that have a scissor bite:

- Basenji
- Border Terriers
- Irish Setters
- Kerry Blue Terriers

Level Bite

A level bite is where the front teeth (incisors) of the upper and lower jaws meet exactly edge to edge. This type of bite may also be called the Pincer bite. The following breeds tolerate a level bite in their Breed Standard but it is undesirable.

- Basset Fauve De Bretagne
- Irish Wolfhounds
- Shih Tzu

Undershot

An undershot bite is where the front teeth (incisors) of the lower jaw projects beyond the front teeth of the upper jaw when the mouth is closed. Quite a few breeds have an undershot bite and here are some examples:

- Boxers
- Bulldogs
- Pekingeses
- Pugs

Overshot

A dog may have an overshot bite, which is when the front teeth (incisors) of the upper jaw overlap and do not touch the front teeth of the lower jaw when the mouth is closed. No breeds should have an overshot bite, this is a fault and would be penalised.

Showing The Teeth

When you are asked to show the teeth, there are 3 steps.

- **Step 1**: gently open the flews on the left-hand side of the dog's mouth and spread them as wide as you can, showing the left teeth. While doing this, tilt the dog's head toward the judge so he does not have to move around to see the left side of the teeth.
- **Step 2**: repeat this action with the right hand side of the mouth.
- **Step 3**: show the bite – gently lift the front flews up with one hand and use your other hand

Showing your dog's teeth

Step 1

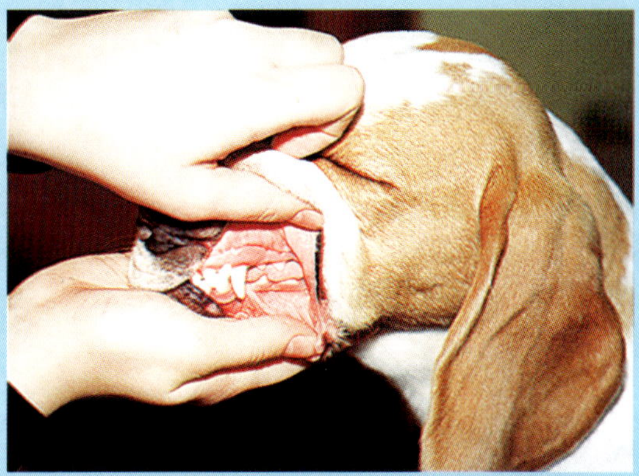

Step 2

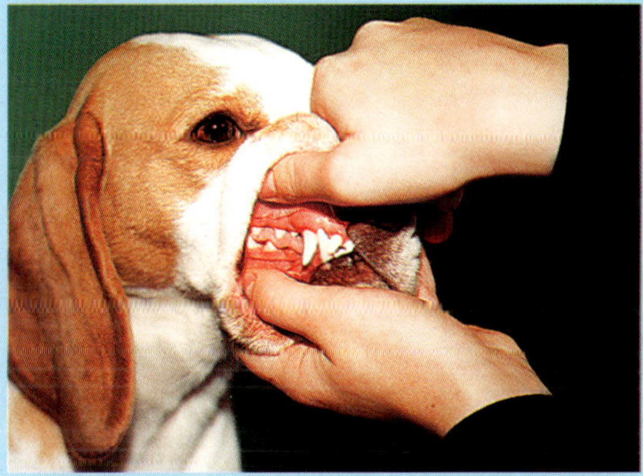

Step 3

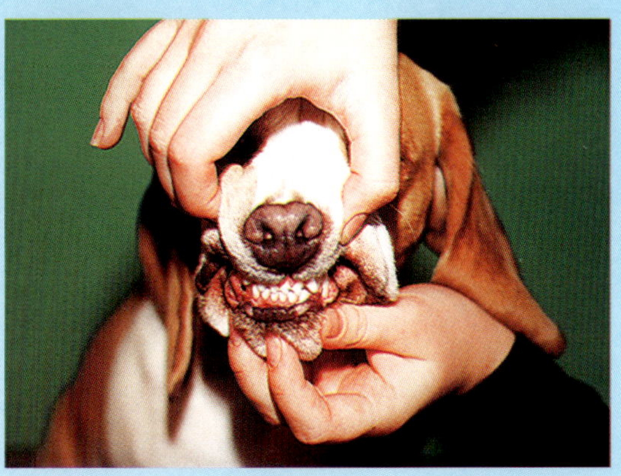

to lower the bottom lip. If asked to show only the bite, complete step 3 only.

The judge may give a nod or say thank you and then the handler should go back to holding the dog as before.

If you are handling a long-coated breed such as a Bearded Collie or a Shih Tzu, remember not to pull the dog's hair around the mouth as this will more than likely cause your dog to back away. Carefully place your fingers in between the teeth and the gums and then spread the lips apart, making sure your dog's hair is neatly tucked away under your fingers.

Conformation

It is essential to have a basic knowledge of a dog's anatomy, because the judge may ask you to point out certain parts of the body. Some handlers and their parents disagree whether there should be any questions asked.

There is no harm in helping to teach handlers a simple understanding of the structure of the dog. Questions asked may include, for example, "Where are the pasterns on your dog?", or "Can you show me where the stop is?"

It is also possible that the judge may want to know a little about your breed and may ask "What was your breed originally bred for?" or "In which country did your breed originate?" The answers to these questions can be found in any corresponding breed book.

Don't let yourself be caught out, so start swatting now! These questions are normally asked when the judge is assessing each handler and dog individually, although some judges may actually ask an anatomy question during the final line-up.

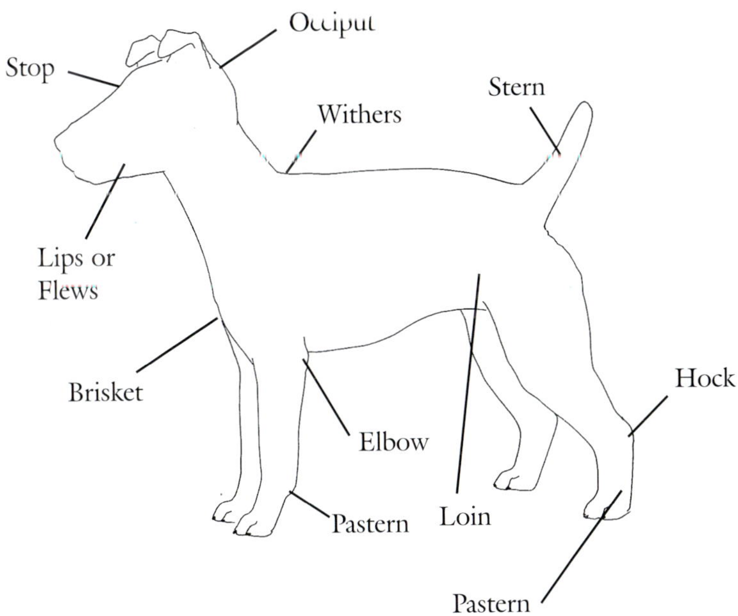

CHAPTER SIX

Learning The Turns

Pattern work is compulsory when competing in a Junior Handling class. The judge needs to see all the dogs in a class move individually, and then together, so then he can assess the handlers' moving capabilities. The patterns are designed so that the judge can see the dog's movement from all angles. However, you need to learn the turns first before embarking on the patterns.

The Golden Rule

The most important rule, when moving your dog for the judge, is not to get yourself in between the judge and the dog. This is known as the Golden Rule. Most of us have made this mistake in competition but, like me, you will remember never to do it again.

Pace

The aim of each pattern in Junior Handling is to test the handler on his ability to achieve the straightest lines, tightest corners and exceptional competence with the dog. For some handlers and their charges this may be difficult because, if your breed is as large as a Standard Poodle, your pace needs to be faster so that you can keep up with him. Consequently, at the corners of certain patterns, or on most turns, you will then need to slow down to achieve the tightest corner. A smaller breed, such as the Lhasa Apso, requires a slower walk because he has a much shorter pace himself, so you cannot go charging away.

Turns

To complete the patterns without breaking the Golden Rule, the handler has to use different turns in order to avoid getting between the dog and the judge.

There are three independent turns, which are called the show turn, the about turn and the inward turn. You need to understand which one to use for each pattern and know how to complete the turn successfully and with confidence.

Training Tip

The easiest way to master each turn and pattern is to start off by practising without your dog. This ensures that you can master the patterns and turns first, before teaching your dog. You will also learn much quicker and your dog will not get so bored.

Go outside into your garden or go to your local park. Put the lead in your left hand and let it dangle to the ground (trying not to touch the floor). Then, tidy up the rest of the lead so it is scrunched up in the palm of your hand. Be careful not to hold the lead with your fist in the air, this is very unprofessional (see pictures in Chapter Four).

Finally, hold your left arm out as far as it can go, parallel with the ground. Then bend your elbow slightly so that your arm feels more relaxed. You should position your arm like this every time you move your dog. You are now ready to study the turns.

The Show Turn

The Show Turn is fairly simple but requires concentration on maintaining balance and walking in a straight line. Use a parent or a friend to imitate the judge, and ask them to stand with their feet together. Then use a cone, or even another person,

The Show Turn Route

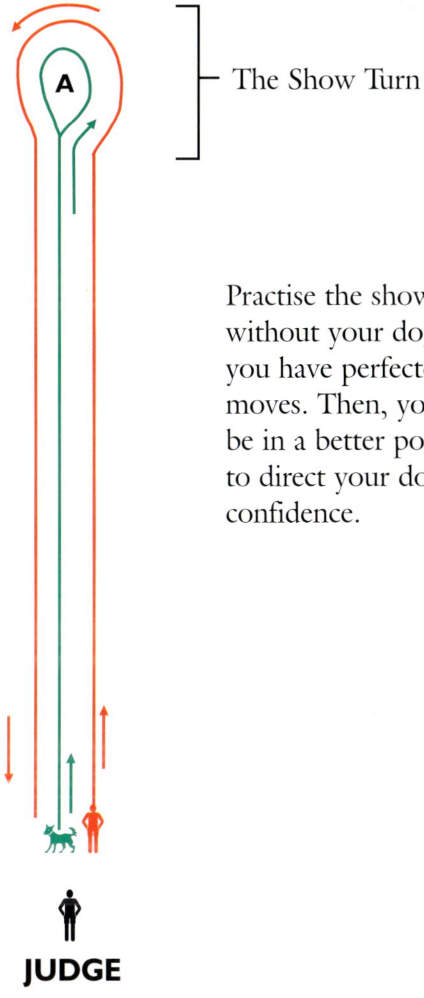

Practise the show turn without your dog until you have perfected your moves. Then, you will be in a better position to direct your dog with confidence.

to stand about three metres in front of the judge. Call this point A.

Now, with your lead in your left hand, stand about one metre in front of the judge and then move one step to the right, so that the lead, not you, is in front of the judge.

SHOW TURN

Correct posture and positioning of the arm and lead before setting off.

Check the judge's position before you turn, so you can adjust your return path.

Walk back towards the judge and your starting position.

Facing point A, begin to walk towards it, making sure that it is the lead which is heading straight to point A and not you. The handler should be about a pace to the right of point A. When the lead is approximately half a metre in front of point A, move to the right of the object and then walk around it. You should end up facing the judge with your back to point A.

Regain the straight line from point A to the judge and walk back towards the judge. Remember, the lead should be in line with the judge and not the handler. Obviously this needs to be practised with your dog as well, but only use your dog when you feel completely confident.

When you eventually train with your dog, practise the show turn without the object at point A being there. Remember that in competition, there is no object there to help you turn. An important detail when walking around point A is to ensure that you keep the dog's pace moving. It looks so untidy and unprofessional if the dog just stops, turns and then strides off again.

Also try to get your turn with the dog tight. This means turning almost on the spot, while remembering to keep the dog's gait moving at all costs.

The Show Turn is used mainly in the up and down.

The Handler: **Annabel Davies**

Annabel comes from Ely in Cambridgeshire, and even though she is only 15 years old, she has already tallied up a tremendous eight years of showing her dogs. Annabel has lived with dogs all her life as her parents have been showing for more than 20 years. She first became aware of Junior Handling classes when she went along to a show with her parents and watched a JHA class. She has also tried Agility and her most memorable occasion was being awarded 2nd prize at a Jersey show. She found this very rewarding as she

Annabel's breed of choice is the Tibetan Terrier

The Tibetan Terrier is stacked on a table for assessment by the judge.

had put so much effort into the event and it was her first time competing in an Agility event.

The Group: **Utility Group**

A collection of breeds that are not classified in any of the other groups.

The Breed: **Tibetan Terrier**

Showing style: ***Table dog***
A Tibetan Terrier is a stacked dog that requires to be set up on the table for the individual pose. The feet must be placed four square and the tail does not need assistance. When on the move, the Tibetan has to be gaited at a moderate pace to enable the dog to make

use of his flowing movement. The coat requires to be brushed downwards to give a good square outline and a brush needs to be taken and used when in the ring. The coat is split into two along the back up to the neck, but on the head some hair is brushed over the eyes to show off the typical Tibetan head. The coat must be left to grow naturally and should never be trimmed.

Other Favourites

Although normally handling a Tibetan Terrier when competing in a Junior Handling class, Annabel has also handled many other breeds including the Russian Black Terrier, Petit Basset Griffon Vendeen, Dachshunds, Poodles, Cocker Spaniels and Whippets.

Dress Sense

When competing, Annabel wears a fitted trouser suit with a white shirt underneath and light-soled shoes. Her hair is always tied back in a neat bun.

Achievements

Annabel has won numerous BJH at Open shows and has also won at Championship shows. In addition to this, she won through to the Pedigree Chum Junior Handler of the Year Finals in 1997 and 1998 and has been the top Tibetan Terrier Junior Handler for the last five years.

It just goes to show that you don't have to go to classes to be successful. Annabel has never attended a ring craft class but was taught all her necessary skills from knowledgeable people in her breed. She wants to thank them, as without all their encouragement and help she would never have got this far.

Memorable Moments

Enjoying the excitement of competing, and her successes, are just two of the elements that Annabel loves about Junior Handling. This attitude has helped her being taken seriously when she is competing against adults in breed showing. She is not too keen on the car travelling involved, although she sleeps most of the way covered in dogs!

Annabel hopes to continue showing her Tibetan Terriers in the breed classes, but hasn't made up her mind whether to follow a career in dogs. It is quite interesting that her school friends do not know that she shows dogs but her out-of-school friends do, and apparently think that she's mad!

Top Tip

Annabel's top tip is never to get nervous when competing, as the dog will then feel nervous too. Stay as calm and relaxed as possible to achieve a focused and purposeful win.

The Switch

Next do this exercise the opposite way around (reverse). This will help you and your dog to achieve all-round balance when moving. This is one detail which handlers do not practise enough.

I have seen it many times before when a handler has had to 'change hands' so that the dog is still in view for the judge. The dog is so used to practising on the left that he is pulling to the left-hand hand side. If I have new puppies in training, I always make sure I am doing as much work on the right as the left.

Large Breeds

Some adult handlers who show large breeds such as the Irish Setter or the Samoyed really let themselves down when it comes to the turns. When performing the Show Turn they nearly always break the Golden Rule by turning to their right instead of the normal left. The dog is more likely to be distracted this way and to my mind you have less control.

There is a way of completing the Show Turn with any large breed. Instead of completing the turn in a sharp, neat circle, pretend there is a shape of a light bulb on the ground and perform the turn in a bigger circle. As long as you get back on line quickly to the judge, the dog's pace will not stop.

The About Turn

The About Turn is similar to the Show Turn but there are a couple of significant differences. This particular turn is used quite frequently when joining two patterns together, so avoiding breaking the Golden Rule. The judge will often ask the handler to complete two patterns one after another, i.e. Triangle (Chapter Seven) then once Up and Down.

This turn should again initially be practised without your dog, just to get familiar with your footwork and lines. Use the same set-up as before, with a person acting as the judge, but this time you don't need a point A.

Stand approximately three metres in front of the judge with the lead in your left hand. Walk towards the judge and, when you get to about one metre in front, move the lead off to the left and then, using a little tension on the lead, bring the dog around you until your back is to the judge. You can either stop completely (not the dog though) when you do the About Turn, or take a step backwards so you do not wobble off balance.

When practising with the dog, make sure that he does not come to a complete stop. Always use

The About Turn

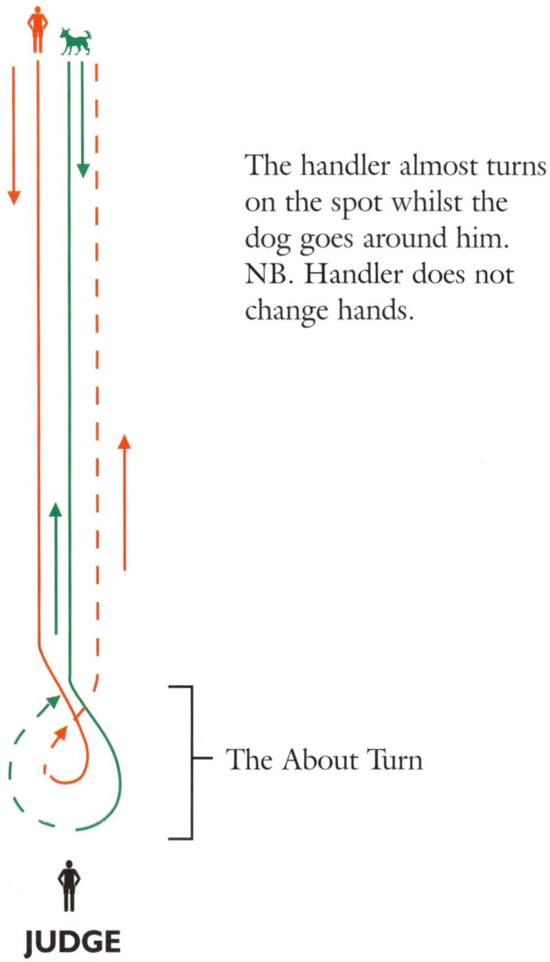

verbal encouragement prior to turning with your dog so that he is forewarned.

The Inward Turn

The last turn to practise is the Inward Turn. This is the most difficult of the three because it requires a considerable amount of concentration, training and balance. This turn is used when the judge has moved his original position (from point A), then the handler has to change hands, in order not to break the Golden Rule.

The Inward Turn may have to be used in an Up and Down, but it is a must in the L and T patterns. Use the same instructions as for the Show Turn, with a friend or parent acting as the judge and then having a point A approximately four metres in front of the judge. I definitely recommend trying this turn initially without your dog, as you need to learn what to do with your hands first.

Change hands swiftly so as not to get between the dog and the judge.

The Inward Turn

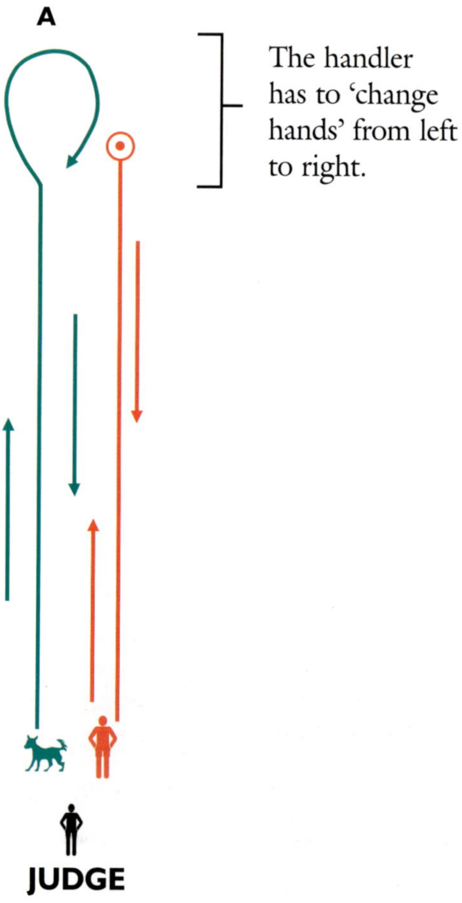

Hold your lead in the position I mentioned earlier and then stand with the lead in front of the judge, facing point A. Walk towards point A, always making sure you are walking in a straight line. Then when you get to point A, stretch your arm out as if to go round Point A. Then bring the lead back towards yourself and change hands, so now the lead is in your right hand. Your hand should be approximately level with your waist throughout the entire exercise. It should be controlled and executed in a slick, neat and tidy manner. Once you feel comfortable with the 'changing hands' part, try it with your dog.

Verbal Encouragement

It is essential to keep the dog's pace going by using verbal encouragement. You need to speak orders like "Turn" or "back", but remember to call the dog's name.

I remember being in a class where one handler had been asked by the judge to do one Up and Down. She ran with her large dog but when she came to turn, the dog just kept going in the same direction. A little verbal encouragement is all you need; you don't need to shout because the dog will respond better if you speak softly.

There was one handler who thought that shouting the loudest and letting the judge hear her screeching was the key to getting a higher placing. She was wrong. Verbal encouragement is expected of all handlers as it shows that you are trying to get the very best out of the dog but there is a limit to the level expected.

Left: A little verbal encouragement when gaiting gives the dog confidence and helps to get the very best from him.

Below: Some dogs simply refuse to move! Be friendly and encouraging to persuade your dog to move with you.

Orientation

Remember to glance back discreetly at the judge a couple of metres before you complete any turn or corner so that you know exactly where the judge's position is at all times. Once you have come back to the judge and presented side-on, the judge may walk around the front or back of the dog, so be prepared to 'shadow' as required. Your dog should be trained to be able to stand in the same position for a short length of time so that you can perform this action efficiently.

CHAPTER SEVEN

The Patterns

There are six separate patterns that you could be asked to perform. No judge will ask you to carry out all six patterns in any one competition, but you will most likely be asked to do two or three. Most judges tend to ask the handler to perform the common patterns that are used in breed showing – the 'circle', the 'up and down' and the 'triangle. These three are the simplest to practise and complete.

- The circle or round the ring
- The up and down
- The triangle
- The letter T
- The letter L
- The figure of 8

The Circle

Most judges tend to ask the handlers for this pattern

Most judges request a 'circle' or 'round the ring' move at the start of the class.

at the start of the class. Primarily, it enables the judge to see the dog's side gait, but in Junior Handling, the judge is looking for a good rapport between the dog and the handler. By this I mean that if the handler is giving the dog enough verbal encouragement, the dog will be responding to that voice. The judge will also look for handlers who are trying to get the best out of their dogs.

As The Circle is almost always the first pattern to be requested, you must impress the judge by looking confident and showing that you are enjoying yourself – but don't go over the top. Many handlers try to impress a judge by smiling fully with brilliant white teeth bared and staring eye to eye. This is unacceptable. It not only looks false but silly too. It really does give a bad impression. However, a good judge will penalise a handler showing off to this extent.

The judge may ask the handlers to go around the ring once or twice. If the class is fairly large, the judge may split the class in two and the first half of handlers would perform The Circle altogether first. Then after they have finished, the second half are told to go around the ring.

If you happen to be first in the line of handlers and the judge asks the class to go "round the ring twice", just move off to your right. If your ring is fairly square shaped, all you have to do is move around the ring with your dog on your left in the shape of a circle.

The Circle

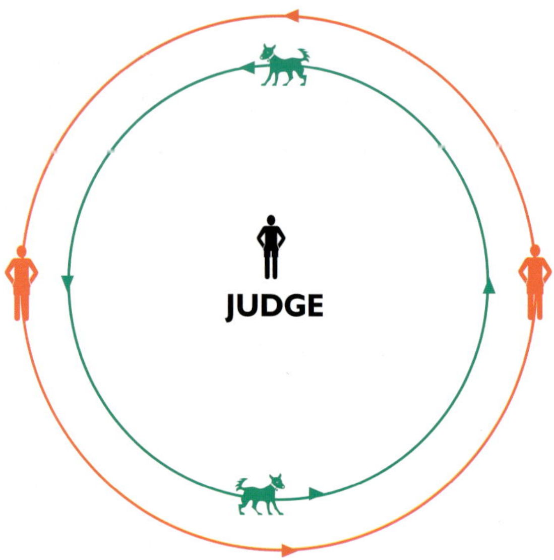

The judge should be standing almost in the centre of the ring and will be watching each handler as they pass. Remember there will be handlers behind you and then you might even catch up with the handlers on the end but don't worry, just keep your eye on the judge and try to keep your dog's pace going continually.

Once you have moved around the ring and have ended up in your original starting position, repeat the circle because, remember, the judge asked you to go around twice. The judge may penalise you if you didn't listen to instructions. It is possible that the judge may move from the centre of the ring, to the edge at any time during The Circle. If this should happen, calmly push the lead with your left hand into your right hand whilst moving around the back of your dog.

It is also very important to keep the dog's pace going so you do not have to slow down or stop to complete the manoeuvre. Your dog should now be on your right-hand side, but then you will find, as you continue on your Circle, that you are breaking the Golden Rule.

Now you need to walk in front of your dog, then do a half turn clockwise whilst changing hands from your right to your left. You should now be on the right hand side of your dog. This can be tricky if not practised properly. Try it at home with just your lead and no dog, as then you can figure out where your feet and hands are going! Some of these moves are difficult. Get someone to demonstrate at your training classes.

The Up and Down

The common Up and Down pattern can be requested more than once during a class. The judge will position himself near the side of the ring so that you have enough room to move. Go to where he is standing and then position your dog about one and

When performing the up and down position, fix on a point ahead so that your lines are as straight as possible.

a half metres in front of him, so you have your back to him.

Make sure you have firm control of your dog, with the lead up behind his ears, and then move off, setting the correct pace for your breed. I always find a point at the other end of the ring to which I keep

Up And Down, Using The Inward Turn

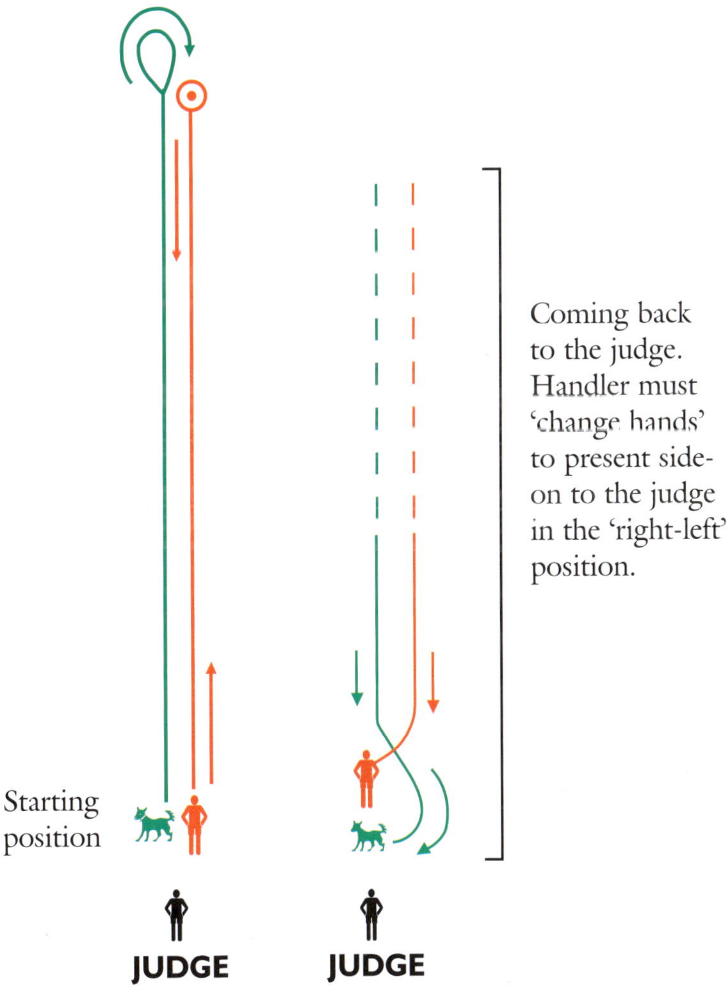

Up And Down, Using The Show Turn

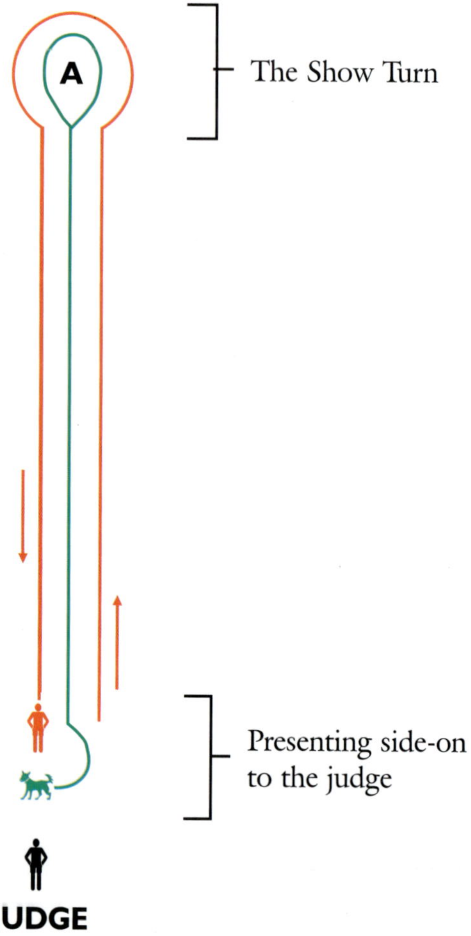

referring so I don't go off line. If you have a breed that is shown on a loose lead, slacken the lead after you move away.

Before you reach the other end of the ring, you need to turn your head around to see if the judge has moved from his original position. If you look back and see that the judge has moved to the right, you will need to perform the Inward Turn. If you find that the judge has either stayed in his original position or moved to the left, you will need to perform the Show Turn.

The judge should never change his position whilst you are on the way back to him. That is bad judging. However, there is a way of getting around this if it does happen to you. It is fairly simple but the dog can often get confused. Let's say that, when you looked back, the judge was in his original position, so you performed a Show Turn but, as you were coming back, he decided to move quickly to the right. Then all you would have to do is use your hand as a guide and steer the dog forward, while you move around the back of the dog. Then change hands and you should be on the left-hand side of the dog.

Presenting Side-on

When you are on your way back to the judge after completing a pattern, you will have to present your dog side-on. This can be accomplished in different ways depending on the judge's final position. If the judge has stayed in his original position and you are about to finish the Up and Down, you need to bring your dog to a halt, about one and a half metres in front of the judge.

If your dog is on your left-hand side when walking back toward the judge, move the dog slightly out to the left and then bring him round side-on. At this point your lead should still be in your left-hand. Quickly but smoothly set up your dog and present to the judge.

At this point, the judge sometimes moves around you and your dog in the stand position so then you are required to 'shadow', as explained earlier. The handler is required to quietly move around the dog, so as not to break the Golden Rule.

Competing Pairs

The judge may ask two handlers to complete the Up and Down pattern together. Trust me, this is a lot easier than it sounds, but can only really work properly if the handlers' dogs move at roughly the same pace. The judge should choose two similar sized breeds to complete this exercise.

Once the judge has positioned himself, the two chosen handlers and their charges should make their way over to where the judge is standing. You might be fortunate because the judge may come behind both handlers in the line up and then ask you to complete the Up and Down together.

Remember to keep the dog in between you and the judge at all times even if you have to walk over

Competing Pairs

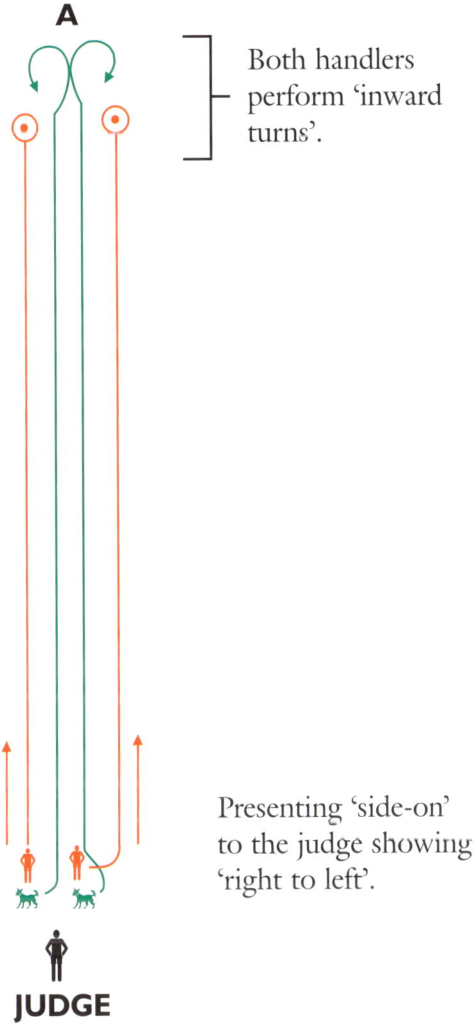

to the judge's starting position. Both handlers should position their dogs on the inside line of the judge's view. For instance, the handler on the left of the judge should have his dog on his right-hand side and the handler to the right of the judge should position his dog on his left-hand side.

Both handlers should make sure that the other is ready to go and then signal to move off in a straight line in front of the judge. Try to leave around 2-3 feet between the two dogs, as the judge wants to keep both dogs in view, but bearing safety in mind.

Once you both reach the far end of the ring and the judge has not moved from his original position, both handlers must complete an Inward Turn to keep the dogs in between you and the other handler. Once you are near to the judge again, the handler on the judge's right-hand side must move around the back of the dog whilst changing hands, then present side-on with the dog's head in the handler's right hand. The handler returning on the judge's left side must bring the dog from his left side to presenting a normal side-on position. Both handlers should complete these last manoeuvres simultaneously and end up with both dogs showing right to left adjacent to the judge, leaving about one to two metres between the dogs and the judge. Remember, the judge could still walk around the back of your dogs, so you need to leave room in between each other for any manoeuvring in and around your charges.

The Triangle

The Triangle is the next most common pattern

The Common Triangle

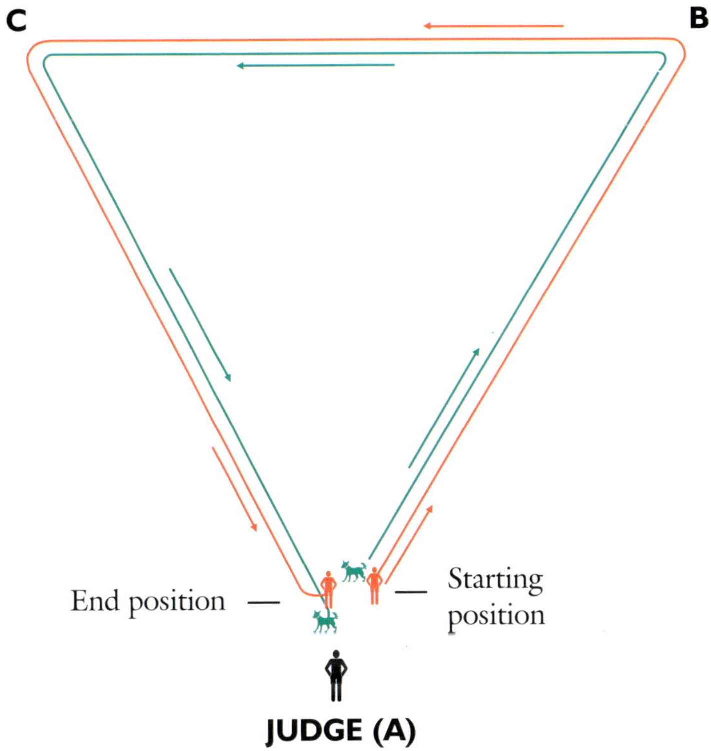

and is quite easy to understand and practise. This pattern is used often in breed showing as it shows the front, side and hind movement of a dog.

Start off in the same position as if you were doing an Up and Down, with the dog on your left-hand side and your back to the judge. This time look at the space in the ring and make sure the dog is facing the right hand corner of the ring. Then move off, making sure the dog is in line between the judge and the corner of the ring you are headed for.

When you reach the corner, shorten your stride, put a little tension on the lead and turn to your left,

Other Ways Of Performing The Triangle

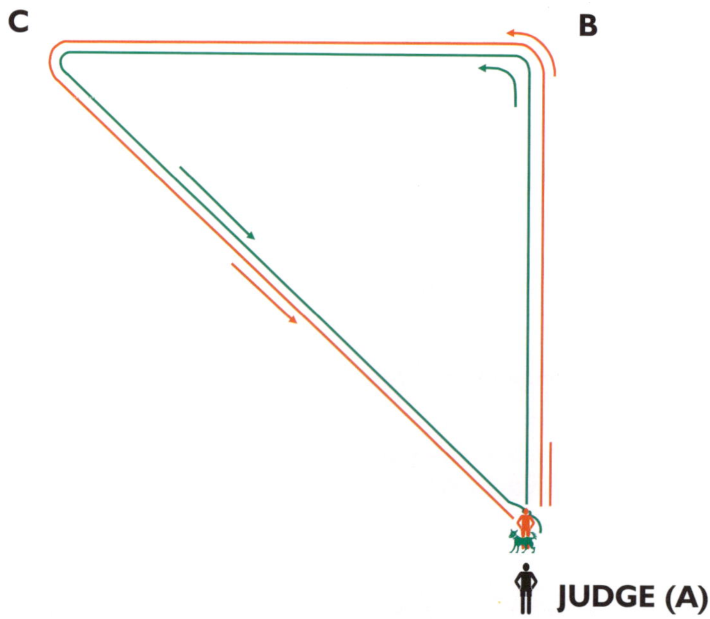

A Common Triangle With A Change In The Judging Position

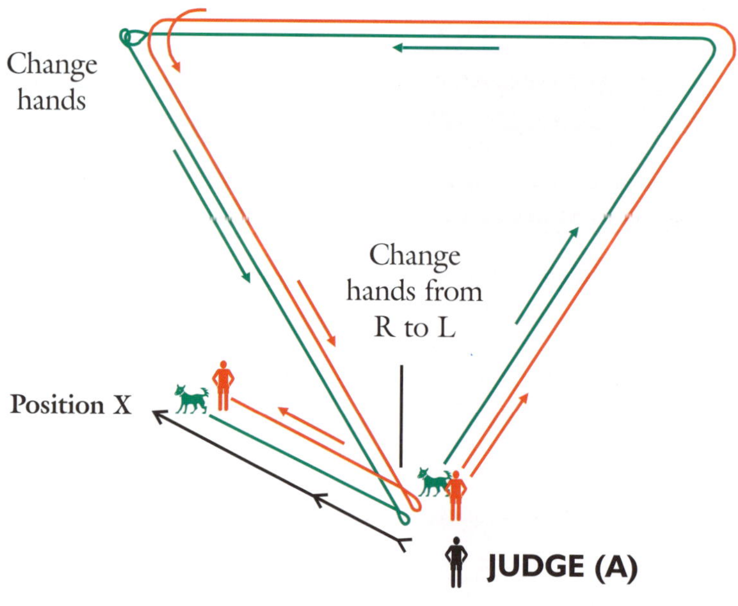

Judge moves to position X when dog and handler are between B & C.

now heading for the other corner of the ring. You should now be side-on to the judge at the other side of the ring.

Again, when you get to the other corner, shorten your pace a little, slow down, put some tension on the lead to slow the dog down and then turn to your left, heading straight back towards the judge.

Once you get near to the judge, you will have to present the dog in the way that I have explained before. In some cases, the judge may move to the left-hand side of the ring position X whilst you are moving from point B-C. If this does happen, perform an Inward Turn at corner C, so then the dog is on your right-hand side, moving back to point A.

If the judge is still at position x, you will need to perform another Inward Turn at point A and then move in a straight line from there to the judge's second position (position x) and present as normal.

Precision Turns

Make clear and precise turns and also make sure you do not stop the dog's pace at each corner. It looks so untidy and unbalanced if the handler 'curves' the corner and the dog starts to pace because he is going too slowly. I am very critical about neat and tidy corners as they are essential to achieving an impeccable Triangle. In one critique, I remember I

Achieving tight turns with a large breed, such as the Great Dane, requires a lot of practice.

wrote about a young boy who had 'curved' his corners so much that it looked as though he had just performed a Circle!

It is much harder to complete a neat corner of a triangle with a dog as large as a Great Dane but a good judge will take into account the size of your dog when performing all patterns. If you do show a large dog, you must train even harder to achieve a tight corner. So, there is no excuse for slackness, whether you show a Chihuahua, a Shetland Sheepdog or an Irish Wolfhound!

Straight Lines

When moving from one corner to another, you must move your dog in a straight line. This might sound easy but if you are trying to control the gait of your dog against your own pace, it is so easy to wobble off line and perform what I call 'banana-shaped lines'!

Again as with most of the turns you have learnt so far, try performing this pattern without your dog, so you know where your feet need to go on the turns and how fast your pace needs to be. At home, I found it easier placing a cone or even a Wellington boot at each corner of my imaginary ring, which I had to move round tightly. Remember you can't put a boot in the ring at the show! The more practice you can get in at home or at training classes, the better.

Avoiding Obstacles

Do remember not to bump into any of the handlers when performing your pattern. If you are asked to do a Triangle, for example, there might be handlers lined up alongside the edge of the ring, so you will have to turn at your first corner a little earlier than predicted so you perform a straight parallel line to the judge.

Reverse Triangle

In Junior Handling classes, the judge may ask for a Reverse Triangle instead, as this requires the handler to show the dog on the right rather than the left. Also the handler is required to head off in the opposite direction from the normal Triangle.

The Reverse Triangle is similar to the triangle that I have just described except it is back to front! Even though it sounds simple, it can be performed quite poorly.

Start off with your dog on your right hand side, with your back to the judge and facing the left corner of the ring. Move off in the direction of corner C, building up the correct pace for your dog. Once you get near to corner C, slow down a little, carefully controlling your dog's pace and then turn

The Reverse Triangle

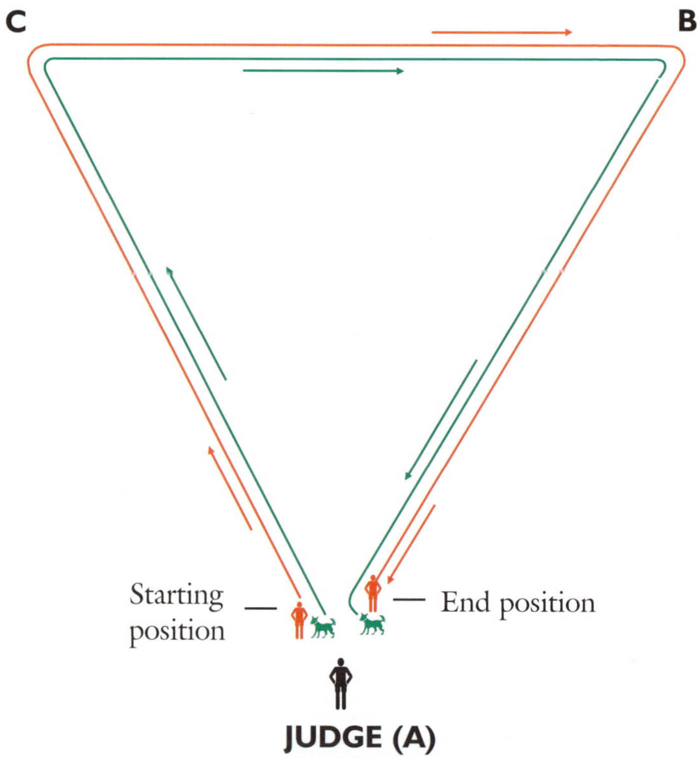

neatly to your right, now moving parallel to the judge. While moving your dog, look back towards the judge, ensuring that he hasn't moved from his original position.

As you approach corner B, remember to slow down slightly the pace of both yourself and your dog so you can turn the corner with balance and precision. You should now be moving directly back towards the judge, with the dog still on your right hand side. As you get nearer to the judge, push the dog's lead with your right hand in front of you, while at the same time moving from the left side of the dog round the back to the right hand side. You then should end up side-on, with adequate spacing between you and the judge, and then present in accordance with your breed.

To complete this last move safely without falling over your dog, you need to give him adequate verbal encouragement and hand signals. This move definitely needs to be practised because it can look awfully untidy, especially with a large breed. If you continued on to the judge with the dog still on your right hand side, you would break the Golden Rule.

The Letter T

The letter T is a more complicated pattern to

understand. There are a number of important points you should be especially aware of when performing this pattern. Straight lines are a must and the Inward Turn has to be very accurate as, in most cases, you will not have very much room. You will probably find that most judges ask for this pattern if they can't decide which of the two class winners is to be Best Junior Handler.

In the older class, the handlers are of a very high standard so I tend to ask them to complete either a letter T or a letter L. This often splits the best handlers from the good handlers.

The Letter 'T'

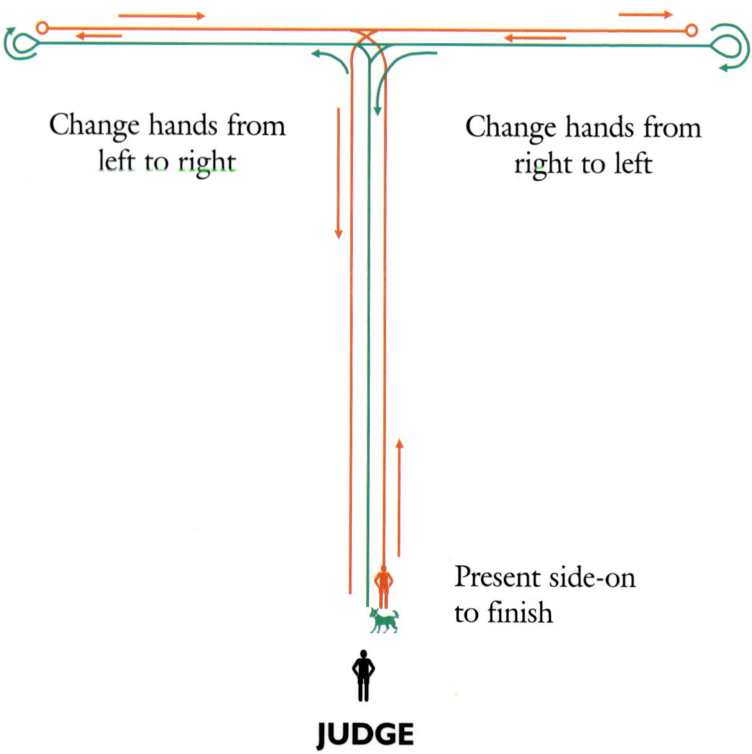

When performing the letter T pattern, the judge should be more or less positioned in the top centre of the ring (the end where the judge would have just finished going over your dog). Start off with your dog on your left-hand side and positioned directly in front of the judge, then move off in a straight line down to the other end of the ring.

Once you reach the edge of the ring, turn neatly to your left with your dog still on your left side. Keep moving forward, parallel to the edge of the ring and, once you get to the corner, perform an Inward Turn. You should now be heading in the opposite direction, toward the other corner of the ring, with your dog on your right side. The judge should remain in his position.

Once you get to the other corner of the ring, perform another Inward Turn and then head back in the opposite direction. Your dog should now be on your left-hand side.

When you reach the centre of the ring, turn sharp left and you should be heading straight back toward the judge. The judge may move slightly right or left while you are performing the T, so you have to check, before you make that last turn toward the judge, that you are in a direct line in front of him before you turn. When on your way back to the judge, remember to complete the pattern and present side on to the judge.

The judge could also ask for a reverse T, which is very similar to the original, with just a couple of variations. When moving away from the judge to the other end of the ring, the dog should be on your right hand side instead of the left and, instead of turning left at the edge, do the reverse and turn right. From then on just do everything in reverse.

The Letter L

The next pattern is the letter L and is performed in a similar way to the letter T. Some judges may want you to begin the manoeuvre in the top corner but some prefer you to start in the centre.

Start off in the same position as described for the letter T, and move in a straight line in front of the judge towards the other side of the ring. Once you reach the other side, turn left toward the far corner, with your dog on your left-hand side, as you did in the letter T pattern.

Again, once you reach the corner, perform an Inward Turn and head back in the opposite direction to the centre. Once you get to the centre or in line with the judge, turn sharp right, now heading straight back towards the judge. Then present as normal.

The letter L can be performed in reverse as well so remember, when a judge asks you to perform

The Letter 'L'

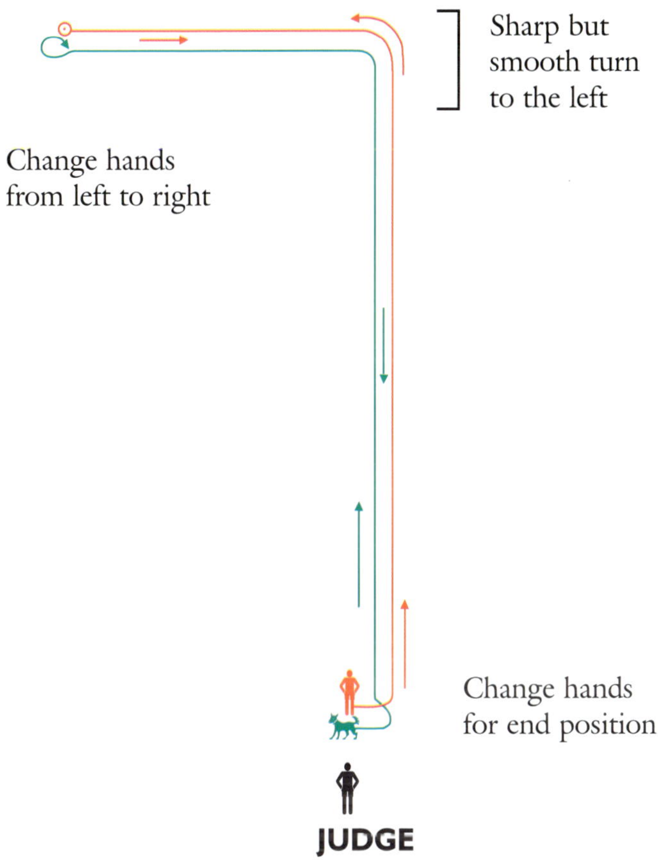

any pattern in reverse, to make sure that, for the starting position, your dog is positioned on your right-hand side.

Tips for Reverse

A little tip to remember is this; think of the two Rs, R for Reverse and R for Right hand side. After you have moved off, going away from the judge, instead of turning to your left when you get to the other end of the ring, turn right and complete the rest of the pattern in reverse. Don't forget the Golden Rule to keep the dog in view for the judge at all times.

The Figure of Eight

The next and final pattern is the Figure of 8. This pattern is by far the most difficult to perform as it involves turning on the move, accurate circles and above all else, a lot of skill. Many judges and Junior Handling specialists alike regard it as too difficult and so this is why it is rarely seen in the handling classes. In my Junior Handling days, I was only ever asked once to do this pattern and I was eight years old at the time. As you can imagine, at that age I didn't perform it too well. Many of you might compete in the handling classes from the age of 6 to 16 and still never get asked. That's how uncommon it is. Still, it is best to show you how to do it, just in case.

The Figure of 8 basically looks like two circles joined together at the middle, so think of the two circles instead of the actual 8 figure when performing. You definitely need to practise this pattern without your dog, because there is a lot of footwork involved that you need to sort out first. There's no point getting both handler and dog confused, when you can at least break it down and get both of you equally confused!

The Figure of '8'

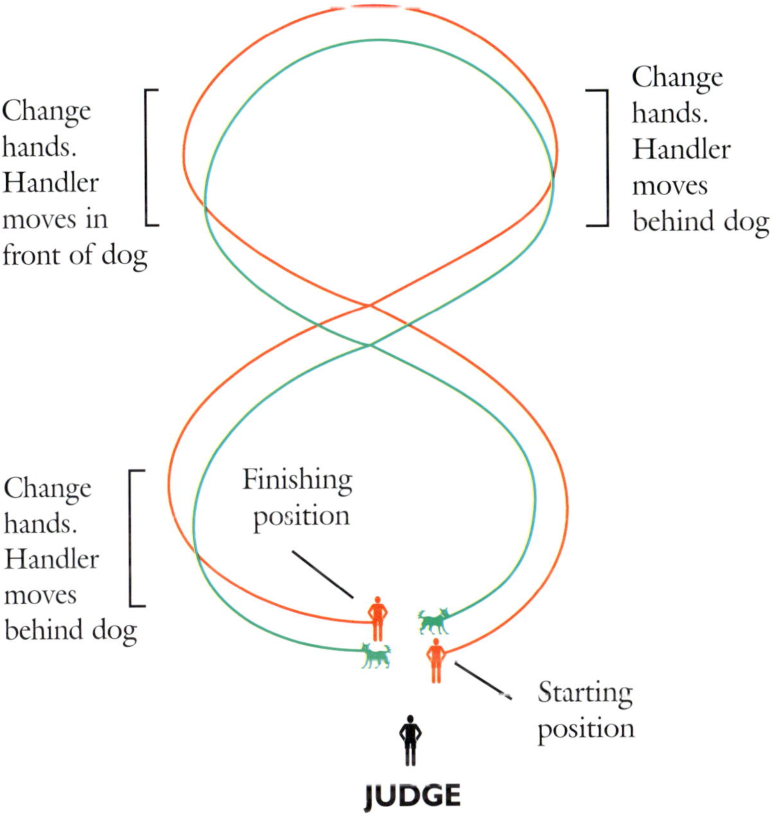

The starting position is exactly the same as for any of the other patterns except that you need to face the right corner of the ring instead of the centre.

The best way to get a perfect pattern is to imagine that you are a spider and, as you move around the ring, your web-line shows where you have been, so that you can adjust your direction to get the perfect circle. This is most useful when it comes to this pattern.

With your lead (no dogs allowed yet!) move off to your right trying to make a semi-circle, then, once you get to the top end of the circle, with your lead still in your left hand, move around to your right thus producing another circle. As you do this, you need to move around the front of the dog and then change hands, so that you are not breaking the Golden Rule.

With your lead now in your right hand, and exactly half way through the exercise, you should be turning slightly to your right. Then you need to move the dog forward faster than your own pace so that you can quickly but tidily nip around the back of him, changing hands in the process.

Your lead should now be in your left hand and you will have completed the top circle. Keep heading in the same direction and then start to turn left and move back toward the judge. As you turn left, you need to push the dog ahead of you by using the lead and verbal commands, while you move around the back of the dog and then change hands.

There are a couple of points that you should remember to try and achieve while performing this pattern. Verbal communication between you and your dog is an absolute must; the more you work on the rapport between yourself and your dog the more precise your patterns will be. Practise,

practise, practise with and without your dog. You want to make it look easy to others and the only way to achieve this is to train yourself so that you could perform it blindfolded!

The Quick Pattern Guide

- When gaiting your dog, move calmly and effectively. Remember that the handler is meant to show off the dog, not themselves.

- Make sure your turns are neat and tidy. No banana-shaped or military style turns. Also, don't forget to keep the dog's pace moving on every corner.

- Straight lines. Nothing is more impressive than seeing a handler and dog moving together in a perfect straight line. Practise at home, walking in straight lines without your dog and then add the dog to complete the perfect duo!

- Remember to keep an eye on the judge. Don't look back every three seconds, but a discreet glance before you make any turn will ensure that you do not break the Golden Rule.

- Verbal commands from you will help the dog understand what you intend to do next. Friendly encouragement is the key to a happy moving dog, because your special words will help your dog relax and pay more attention.

The Handler: **Charlene Kirk**

Charlene, aged 19 and from Lincolnshire, has been involved with dogs since she was very young and she competed in her first handling class when she was six years old. She hopes to continue her dog interest as a judge for breed and Junior Handling classes. She also wants to pursue a career in Customs and Excise using drug sniffer dogs.

The Group: **Gundog Group**

A group of breeds that find and catch feathered and furry game. Setters and pointers indicate where birds are, Retrievers fetch hares and rabbits and birds which have been shot, Spaniels do both jobs.

Charlene has enjoyed great success in handling the English Springer Spaniel.

The Springer is a stacked floor dog.

The Breed: **English Springer Spaniel**

Showing style: ***Floor dog***

The Springer is a stacked breed with both front and back feet being positioned level, which means four-square. When stacking this breed, it is essential to achieve a level top line, which means that the tail must be held level with the dog's back. This breed is moved at a moderate pace, but sometimes the pace depends on the dog himself. The Springer does not require any special grooming, but does need regular bathing and trimming, especially before every show. The trimming is done on the ears, neck, feet and below the tail, but never on the topcoat. If the Springer has excess topcoat, this can be stripped out using a stripping knife.

Other Favourites

Charlene has handled a few other breeds in competition including the German Shepherd Dog, a Weimeraner, Whippets and Bedlington Terriers. She would like to show Border Collies, who are intelligent and loyal, the smart and stylish Hamiltonstovares, and Schnauzers which are eye-catching and powerful movers.

Dress Sense

When handling in any competition, Charlene normally sports a smart trouser suit in a colour which complements the dog she is showing at the time. She wears a flat pair of shoes which are suitable for moving at a fast pace.

Achievements

In the year 2000 Charlene was awarded the two top handling titles in the UK. In the January she won the Pedigree Chum Junior Handler of the Year award and then, two months later, at Crufts she did the double and was awarded the KCJO Show Handler of the Year title.

Memorable Moments

The best has to be winning the two major titles in one year, but coming a very close second was rearing her dog's first litter of puppies.

She also remembers attending a local open show

Winning the Pedigree Chum Junior Handler of the Year award has been a highlight in Charlene's handling career.

with her family, where one of the competitors in the 6-11 years class was completely unable to control her dog, upset everyone around her, but still won. Apparently the judge was only about 10 years old, with his father acting as steward – but actually doing most of the judging as well!

Charlene's friends find her hobby slightly strange, involving, as it does, getting up at two in the morning to drive to some far-off place, running the dogs round the ring once and then spending the rest of day doing very little in wind, rain and hail!

Top Tip

Charlene enjoys the general excitement of handling and the socialising, with the many friendships she has formed. The worst part is the travelling, particularly if it has been a bad day and the mood in the car is solemn.

Her best tip is always to be yourself.

CHAPTER EIGHT

Show Day

Make sure both you and your dog are well prepared by using a check list, and make as many advance preparations as you can. Get as much as possible packed into your car the night before. Try to be even more prepared by polishing your shoes and laying all your clothes out, so you can quickly put them on in the morning, especially if you are leaving early.

If you are going to a Championship show, it is essential that you remember your show passes, that would have been sent to you prior to the show. Use a plastic envelope for all your paperwork – the show passes, the schedule and the proof of posting certificate – to keep everything together and dry. It will save a lot of stress and hassle.

Chains, Cages and Seats

Most General Championship shows are 'benched', so you don't necessarily need a cage. Instead you

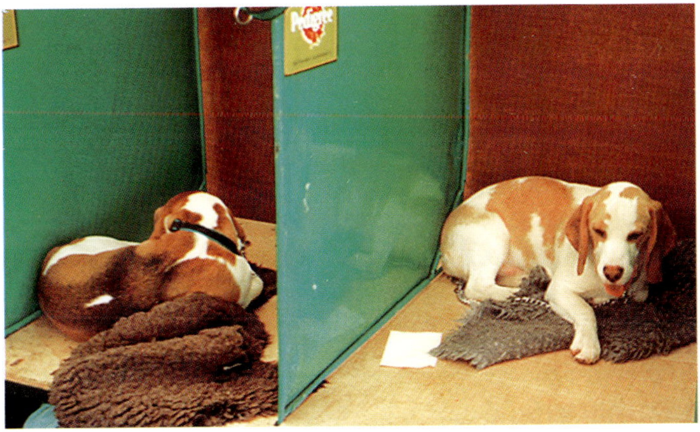

Don't forget a benching chain if you are handling at a Championship Show.

use a benching chain which hooks from the dog's collar to specially designed benches.

We also take the cage, because I prefer the dogs to be secure and warm. Some cages, however, may not fit on the benches, which are supposed to be big enough for the breed, but sometimes can be quite small.

It is always useful to take a couple of folding-down chairs as, at most shows, there is limited seating available.

Travel Arrangements

When travelling to your show, your dog or dogs should be caged, or be in the boot with a dog guard. This will keep them safer, in case you have to suddenly stop. Too often I see careless owners driving about town, or even along the motorway, with their dog standing on the back seat peering out of the half-open window.

It is always better to be safe than sorry. The dog obviously does not know what's right and what's wrong as far as his safety is concerned, so you have to show him the right thing to do.

If your family car is a hatchback and has the dog in the back, that's fine, but if your dog hasn't been trained to stay where he is when you open the boot, this could unfold into quite a dangerous situation. You might want to fit a specially designed cage, which has a door that you can open separately after you have opened the boot.

Additional Equipment

Take a map, an umbrella, a torch and a warm rug just in case you break down. Also remember a couple of doggy towels to wipe down your dog when you get to the show, especially if it has been raining.

The Picnic Basket

You will find that you will be at the show for the best part of the day so, at some point, you will obviously get hungry. My mum and I found that because I eat so much all the time, it was getting far too expensive and unhealthy to keep eating burgers and chips all day. Now, we take a picnic bag full of snacks such as fruit, whole-grain bars and a flask of hot water for tea. It is much easier than having to wait around outside in the freezing cold in a huge queue.

Timing Your Arrival

Make sure you leave yourself plenty of time to get to your destination. Allow for accidents, traffic jams and weather conditions.

An hour is quite sufficient time to get to the show before your judging is scheduled to start. For example, if the judging says 9.30am start, aim to arrive by 8.30am.

Safety Tip

Never, ever leave your dog in a car, even if it is only a slightly warm day. The temperature in a car can rise very quickly. Show officials are very strict about leaving dogs in cars on hot days, especially at Championship shows, and will, if necessary, break into cars to rescue dogs in distress. The best rule is never to leave dogs in cars, whatever the weather; it is totally unfair on them.

The Handler: **Shona Taylor**

Shona, a consistent and knowledgeable winner from Aberdeen, Scotland, has been handling since the age of four. She first became involved in showing dogs when she used to go along with her Gran to training classes. One day when she was watching intently, she was offered a Rough Collie to handle and as soon as she was up moving and standing the dog, she was hooked! The gentleman who owned the dog said she was a natural and, when he sadly passed away, she was given one of his other Rough Collies to show. Up until a few years ago, Shona mainly handled her Shih Tzu in Junior Handling, but then she bought a Chinese Crested puppy and handled that breed in the competition thereafter.

The Group: **Toy Group**

Includes the smaller breeds which are not to be regarded as ladies' pets.

The Breed: **Chinese Crested Dog**

Showing style: ***Table dog***

The Chinese Crested Dog has two varieties within the breed: powder-puff and the hairless. A Chinese Crested Dog is moved at a moderate pace which requires the handler to walk reasonably quickly. As a small dog, the Crested is examined by the judge on the table. On the table Shona stabilises the dog by 'stringing up'. When on the floor, the Crested is free-stood four-square and is baited to keep his ears

Shona with Paige, a powder-puff Chinese Crested Dog. Photo: Alan Walker.

erect. As Shona's dog is a powder-puff, a comb or brush is required in the ring to tidy up any straggly hairs after moving. She adds that some judges think that making a squeaky noise will encourage the dog to put his ears up, but with her Chinese Cresteds this has the opposite effect. Her dogs think that you want to play!

Other Favourites

Shona has also handled many other breeds from the Cocker Spaniel to an Irish Setter, a Cavalier King Charles Spaniel (CKCS) to a Tibetan Terrier, a Pug to a Great Dane. In fact she has handled over 40 different breeds spanning every group! Her favourite three breeds are the Pointer, Afghan and Staffordshire Bull Terrier. She loves the Pointer's movement, plans to buy an Afghan in the future and thinks that the Staffy looks as if he is always smiling!

Dress Sense

Shona normally sports black trousers, black top and shoes with a smart blue jacket on top, when she is handling in the ring. In addition her hair is tied back.

Achievements

Shona's experience of handling many different breeds has brought her much success, including being the Scottish Junior Handler of the Year winner in 2000 after being runner-up for the previous four years! Her other successes include being the 8-11 year class winner at the KCJO Show Handler of the Year Finals at Crufts in 1996 and then being a finalist four times as well. She has also made it into the Pedigree Chum Junior Handler of the Year finals twice.

Having now outgrown Junior Handling, Shona continues to show her own Shih Tzus and Chinese Cresteds in breed competitions but hopes to become either a professional handler or to work with animals in some way in the veterinary field.

Memorable Moments

Her most memorable occasion was winning the Scottish Junior Handler of the Year title as she was beginning to think that she would never achieve beyond 2nd!

Her most humorous situation was when she was watching a 6-11 years class and a young girl handling a large dog got pulled off her feet and dragged out of the ring on her face. She eventually returned to the ring, covered in mud from head to toe, and then was placed first! Apparently the judge's critique said that "the young girl had a hard dog to control but coped well." The worst thing was that this was at a Championship show.

Her school friends think highly of her hobby, especially when she has won, but don't really understand what is involved. Apparently they think 'handling' means that her dogs jump through burning rings of fire!

She manages to find time to attend two ring craft classes but only one of them includes a separate time for the juniors, which is at the beginning of the evening.

Top Tip

Shona generally loves being in the ring doing the patterns and thinking quickly when the judge asks questions. The worst part, for her and so many handlers, is the travelling, particularly when you live in Aberdeen and the nearest Championship show is two and a half hours south!

Her top tip is always to listen to the judge so that you know what is being asked of you and to learn to become just as good a loser as you are a winner.

Example of a Show List

Date of show	7/1/01	20/1/01	10/2/01	4/3/01	10/4/01
Show lead and collar	√				
Short walking lead	√				
Benching chain					
Cover for cage	√				
Bedding					
Dog towels	√				
Dog bowl					
Dog food	√				
Grooming bag/box					
Bottle for water					
Titbits	√				
Winter coat					
Scarf					
Gloves					
Wellington boots					
Map					
Sunglasses					
Mobile phone					
Headache tablets					
KCJO book					
Show schedule					
Show clips					
Show jacket and shoes					
Picnic bag					
Poo bags					

Arriving At The Show

At nearly all Open shows, the Junior Handling is scheduled either at lunchtime or in the first available ring (which is normally after lunchtime). Championship shows work slightly differently. They cover a much larger area of ground and the car park may be some considerable distance away from your benching area.

Take all your bags, and your dog, straight into the show. Remember to have your passes ready because you have to show them to the officials at the actual show ground entrance. Poo bags need to be handy. Some Championship shows send out special coloured car park passes in addition to your show ground passes. If you have been sent a car park pass, put it on the inside of the front window so the officials can quickly let you pass and get parked.

Inside The Ground

Once you and your dog have entered the show ground, there are normally show officials who will point out your specific benching tent. Inside the large benching tent there are many wooden benches lined up in parallel, with numbers above each of them.

On your show pass, the official should have let you keep the part that includes your dog's number. Look at the number and look for your matching bench number. The benching tents can sometimes get rather crowded and tight for space, so watch your dog when walking in between the benching. Some breeds are renowned for guarding their benches, so make sure you have a firm grip of the lead.

Catalogues

After you have settled your dog on his own bench, you may choose to buy a catalogue. This lists all the entries in each class on your day of the show and gives you space underneath to write down the winners and absentees. The judging follows the order of the catalogue, but this can be changed at the discretion of the show management.

It is possible to order a prepaid catalogue on your entry form, but you will only be able to pick it up on the day of the show. It is often cheaper if you pay for the catalogue this way.

Trade Stands

At Championship shows and most Open shows, there will be many different trade stands offering

Trade stands sell everything a dog owner needs.

dog food, agricultural goods, grooming products etc. Most of these stands travel round to nearly all the Championship shows during the year, so if you forget to buy something, there is always the next show. But try not to get too carried away with the shopping part so that you miss your class. I always have a potter around the stands after I have competed in my class, so that way I'm not missing anything I shouldn't!

Dog Care

Keep checking on your dog at least every half an hour, especially if he is on his own. Take him for a short walk about half an hour prior to your class so, if he takes longer to do his toilet than usual, you are not going to be stressed about missing your class. It is dreadful when you have to rush into the ring, all flustered, knowing that your dog still needs to spend a penny!

The Last Moments

You might start feeling a little nervous before you go into the ring. I still do now! You will eventually find your own way of handling this situation. For instance, about 5 to 10 minutes before I am about to enter the ring, my Mum has to leave me completely alone because I just like focussing and concentrating on the task ahead. For the entire morning, Mum can tell me things that I need to remember, but the few minutes beforehand is my time and it's great, because she understands!

Before your class is called, leave yourself enough time for last minute tasks like grooming, putting titbits in your pocket, putting the show lead on your dog and pinning the ring number to your jacket (if at a Championship show).

If your dog is a long-haired breed, he would have had considerable grooming before the day of the show. If your dog is a short-haired breed, he still does need a quick groom just to achieve that extra sparkle.

The Call To The Ring

At Open shows, you need to look in the catalogue to see what number or letter you are. Remember this information, because you will need to ask for this card when you are called into the ring by the steward.

The Junior Handling classes at Open level are often called out over the speaker system as, sometimes, the ring changes and there is no specific time. At Championship level, the Junior Handling classes often have their own specific time and designated ring. The classes at this level are also often called out over the speaker system so absentees will be kept to a minimum.

Once you are outside the ring with your dog, wait patiently for the steward to call out either "Junior Handling 6-11 years" or "Junior Handling 12-16 years".

Inside The Ring

Walk into the ring and ask the steward for your ring number or letter, which you should already know from the catalogue. Pin it on to your clip and then walk over to the side of the ring, which is to the left of the table.

The steward will tell you where to go, and possibly ask for all the large breeds to be lined up first, with the smaller breeds following them. As soon as you walk into that ring, you are going to try and impress the judge as much as possible. Smile and look happy, as this will get noticed, particularly when compared with an unhappy, solemn youngster.

Watch the judge's position even when you are collecting your ring card, because you might break the Golden Rule.

Choosing Position

Choosing your position in the first line-up is important, because some handlers prefer to be last and some first. I always like to position myself around about second or third, because this gives me a chance to see what patterns the judge might ask for. Also, I hope I can make a good impression early on for the judge so then the rest of the handlers have to try to outshine my performance!

You will find that, when the class is called in, most of the handlers will hesitate and wait for someone else to go in first. Don't let this put you off. Even if you go in first, you can wait until someone else follows and then quietly slip in behind them. Don't ever push or shove, as this will be noted by the judge.

Make sure you are lined up in the line-up!

Leaving Space

Once you have got your place, leave enough space between the dog and the handler on both sides of you, as you need room to set up your dog, and move around him, if necessary. Glance down both ends of handlers and set your dog up in a straight line with all the other dogs.

The First Movements

By this time the judge might be walking up and down the line of handlers and you should watch his movements and listen for any given instructions.

The judge may then ask for a "Circle", or "Round the ring once/twice", so wait until the handler in front moves off and then follow on behind.

You should try to make as much use of the ring space without continually touching the edges. Some rings may be quite rectangular, but just use common sense and achieve the best circle you can in the available space.

Remember to keep glancing back at the judge to see if he is still in the same position and be prepared if he moves to the edge of the ring. Once you have completed the exercise, gently come to a stop, still showing off your dog, as the judge may like to see how you come to a halt.

Individual Assessment

The judge will then beckon the first handler in the line to go onto the floor or table, depending on the breed. At this point, if you are still standing in the line, keep your dog attentive but composed, as the judge may glance at him at any time during the class.

Whilst you are waiting, assess the ring space and look for any uneven bumps in the ground. Watch what patterns the previous handlers have been asked to do and whether the judge moves position at all. Remember that the judge might not ask for the same patterns every time, but it is usually the case.

Remain calm and relaxed while the judge is assessing your dog.

When the handler directly in front of you in the line is performing his patterns, you must then put your dog on the table or on the floor and set him up unless directed to do otherwise by the steward or the judge. Ideally, when the judge looks around after assessing the previous handler, he wants to see you and your dog ready in the show pose.

The Pattern Work

After the judge has finished assessing your dog, he will then beckon you, or simply ask you to complete a pattern. The judge will move over either to the centre of the ring or to a corner and so follow him, remembering to keep the dog between you and the judge. At this point, a lot of handlers still forget to make sure they are not breaking the Golden Rule, even when walking from the table or floor to the judge's starting position. If you have carried out your pattern training programme, you should be prepared for any pattern asked.

On completing the pattern, the judge will then thank you and tell you to rejoin the end of the line. Say a polite "thank you" back and move off, heading round the ring towards the end of the line. A good handler should always be polite to the judge, and thanking the judge at this point will show respect.

This is your round completed but always continue to show the dog when moving back to the end of the line as, sometimes, the judge may still be watching you. It is very disappointing, after a really good round, to see a handler walking back and looking about the ring as if to say "ha, ha I've finished!", not realising that the judge is still watching him.

The Waiting

Once you are back in the line of handlers, keep your dog alert but not in show pose, just in case the judge tries to catch you unaware. Spare a thought for the other handlers who are performing their patterns. Keep your dog under control and as far into the side of the ring as you can as the other handlers and their charges go past.

Keep an eye on how many handlers are left to be seen as, once the last handler is performing his pattern work, you will need to start setting your dog up into show pose. At this point the judge will again walk up and down the line watching each and every handler. Remember to keep reassuring your dog by speaking softly and frequently.

The Judging

If the class contains as many as 15 handlers, the judge may choose to pick out a further 6 or 7

The steward or judge will hand out rosettes to those that are placed.

handlers for reassessment. If the class is quite small in number, the judge may just pick out the winners immediately.

If the judge cannot decide, even in a small class he still might reduce the class size to four or five and then ask each handler to perform another pattern. The key at this stage is to watch and listen very carefully as you might miss the judge pointing at you to be pulled out into the last few.

Once the judge has reassessed you and the rest of the handlers, he will then make his decision and start pulling each handler out, starting with first place right down to fourth or VHC (very highly commended or fifth). If you are picked out first, walk out into the middle of the ring, or to where the steward directs you to go.

At this point, don't forget the Golden Rule but begin to set up your dog again. The other handlers who have been picked in consecutive order will now be lining up alongside you. Keep showing at this stage, as the judge still has the right to swap you around if he feels it necessary.

Not until the judge gives a nod, or tells the steward the placings, can you relax but, if I were you, I would still show, until the steward shouts out something like "the winner of class 236, Junior Handling 6-11 years is letter S".

People outside the ring will start clapping and you will then receive any rosettes, cards and/or specials by the steward. The steward may then ask you to stay in the ring (if you won the older age group class) or come back after the judging of the older class has finished (if you won the 6-11 years class) as you will have to compete for Best Junior Handler. Give your dog a well-earned pat or stroke on the back and then you may leave the ring.

Winning

If you were fortunate enough to have won a Junior Handling class, the club or society may award a Best Junior Handler on the day. This means that you have to go up against the winner of the other Junior Handling class. At most Championship shows you

The 6-11 years' class winner competes against the 12-16 years' winner for the Best Junior Handler title.

Junior handling trophies and cups are on offer at some shows.

will find that there is no award for Best Junior Handler but at nearly all Open shows there is.

After both classes have been judged, the two winners will be asked to go back into the ring to compete for Best Junior Handler. Again, set up your dog as if you were competing in your class but this time you really have to sparkle and make sure you don't make any silly mistakes.

The judge may ask you to do a number of different patterns, either working alongside the other handler (circle or up and down together) or without. He will try to catch you out at this stage so remember to keep glancing back every so often when performing your patterns.

The judge will essentially be looking for a good rapport, excellent technical ability and nice presentation. Smiling and looking happy will help not only yourself but also your dog. You must listen very carefully to what the judge says and keep an eye on what the other handler has been asked to do.

The steward will probably give the judge a rosette especially for the handler that wins the overall award. At this point the judge will walk over to the winner and shake their hand. Then the judge should still congratulate the runner-up. The judge may ask the two winners, with the Best Handler overall going first, to move around the ring together while the spectators clap.

If you are a member of the KCJO, don't forget to get your KCJO book signed after the judging of the handling classes by either the judge or the steward. Check to see if there is a Best Junior Handler trophy or cup, because some shows forget to tell you. Unfortunately, most of these trophies have to go back at the next show or the following year so always keep them clean for the next winner.

Show Records

When you get home, whether you were not placed or got a first, update your show record. This should include details such as the name of the show, date, class, judge, your placing, number of entries, any qualifications and any trophies collected. I have always recorded this way and it helps when I recognise a judge's name and can look up my records to see if I have previously been under him or her.

A Show Record

Show	Date	Class	Judge	Placing	Entries	Qualifications/Trophies?
LKA	*14/12/01*	*12-16*	*Joe Bloggs*	*2nd*	*11*	*J. H. A. diploma*

Show Day Hints

- Pack as much as you can into the car the night before.
- Take a picnic including fruit and flasks of tea/coffee.
- Buy a catalogue, then you can find out how long you have got to go until your class.
- Leave plenty of time between getting your dog ready and going into the ring.
- Keep a show record of your wins and placings.
- Do not leave your dog in the car, whatever the weather.

CHAPTER NINE

Sportsmanship and Etiquette

The world of dog shows provides many people with an enjoyable and entertaining hobby and leads to the excitement and uncertainty of competition against like-minded individuals. This special atmosphere is only possible if certain standards of behaviour are observed by all competitors.

Sportsmanship

This can best be defined as displaying a fair and good-humoured attitude to everyone, irrespective of the result.

For Junior Handlers in particular, it is essential to display sportsmanship and to encourage a friendly yet competitive atmosphere in and around the ring. When competing at any dog show, you will come across a whole range of characters and personalities that you, personally, may or may not like. Never let this influence your own behaviour. Each and every handler has to cope with the pressures of winning and losing in their own way, and sometimes it is very hard.

The Wrong Way

I found it most difficult to accept not being placed higher when I first started handling. When I was aged about 9, I competed in the 6-11 years class at a local Open show in Aberdeen. I had not been showing very long, but when I was only placed fourth, I felt I was hard done by and came out of the ring crying. Looking back, that was the worst thing I could have done. The class entry was high and the quality of the handling was very good, therefore a fourth was a respectable placing against tough competition.

The Right Way

My mother taught me how to appreciate each and every placing, whether it was a first, or no placing at all, by learning the phrase 'Win with pride but lose with dignity'. I have used this motto ever since and it definitely gets easier with age and experience.

Even now, when I'm showing in the breed ring and I don't get the placing I felt I deserved with my dog, I might be a little disappointed but I congratulate the winner with a smile and leave the ring with a smile. I find that once I have congratulated the winner, all my disappointment disappears. I realise that it was just another class, and that there is always another day and another show!

Always congratulate the winner because it shows you are mature and have graciously accepted the judge's decision. Just say something like "Well done" or "Congratulations" and give a touch or a pat on the back. The winner will most certainly appreciate the gesture. If on the other hand, you are the winner, you will appreciate it when your fellow competitors approach you and say "Well done".

The more you compete, the more you will start to recognise fellow handlers and, with time, many could become close friends. This is one of the reasons why acting in a sportsmanlike manner from the start will help you become a worthy competitor.

The Unacceptable

One thing you must never ever do is ask the judge why you were placed where you were. I have seen this happen, and it is quite unacceptable, especially when a mother has told her child to go up and ask. If the judge approaches you and explains why, that is fine, but never argue, because the decision has already been made.

It is very frustrating when you feel you have done your best and were not placed higher. This decision could possibly be due to poor judging but, far more likely, it is because you did something wrong that you may not have noticed. It is useful if your mum, dad or a friend watches your round and then can comment on your performance afterwards. That might answer some of your questions.

Etiquette

Another attitude-related subject is etiquette. This basically refers to matters such as cleaning up your dog's mess, and being polite to the judge, to fellow competitors and keeping control of your dog.

Distractions

Arriving late for your class and barging in front of other handlers is a good example of bad etiquette, as is distracting another handler's dog while he is being assessed on the table.

Gossip

One thing that you must never do is talk to other

handlers in the ring, unless it is absolutely necessary. I watched a handling class a year or two ago and noticed two girls having such a deep conversation that they failed to spot that the judge was waiting for one of them to set up their dog on the table. Eventually a lady from outside the ring had to tell them. It was really rather funny, but the girl did look rather embarrassed afterwards when her Mum had a few words with her.

You should be concentrating on your composure and keeping the dog relaxed but still in show demeanour, just in case the judge looks down the line at you. Save the chat until after the competition.

Poop Scoops

Throughout your showing career, it is quite possible that your dog may foul the ring, if he is not exercised adequately prior to the competition. Not all societies provide sufficient facilities such as buckets and shovels. If your pockets are large enough, carry a small plastic bag so you can clear it up yourself. Most often a good steward will be quite willing to help but do not disrupt the handler being assessed at the time.

Control

Keep your dog under control at all times in the ring. Do not let him jump all over other dogs or juniors! There is nothing worse than being on the receiving end of this unnecessary behaviour, and having muddy footprints imprinted on your bright blue jacket. If you cannot physically control your dog on your own, then consider handling a different breed that you can cope with.

The Good Behaviour Guide

- Always congratulate the winner of your class.
- Carry a plastic bag in your pocket for any mishaps.
- Keep control of your dog at all times.
- Pick up any titbits or objects on the floor you may think might distract your dog, or another handler's dog.
- Don't distract other handlers and dogs by talking too loudly or throwing titbits.

The Handler: **Katie Hamilton**

Katie, now aged 14, from Scotland, has been handling since she was six years old. Her interest was kindled by the fact that her mother was showing dogs and she would watch the classes being judged. Her future hopes include continuing showing, but her dream is to become a vet.

Lively and spirited, the Border Terrier is no easy dog to handle, but Katie enjoys the challenge that the breed presents.

The Group: **Terrier Group**

The terriers vary in size and are bred to seek out and catch small rodents.

The Breed: **Border Terrier**

Showing style: ***Table dog***

Katie says that it is much more difficult than it looks handling Border Terriers, as they would rather be outside chasing rabbits. Although the dogs' gait may vary from one to another, in general Katie says you should walk quite swiftly with a Border.

In Handling competition, she prefers to stack her dog, as this allows her better lead control and she can shadow more easily. However, when in breed showing, she tends to free-stand her dog because it shows the dog off well.

The Border requires hand-stripping twice a year, which should result in a harsh and dense coat with a close undercoat. Never trim the Border's coat; this can only be done on the feet and the tip of the tail.

Other Favourites

Katie has shown many other breeds including the Airedale Terrier, the Golden Retriever, Whippets, Smooth Fox Terriers, a Siberian Husky, Staffordshire Bull Terriers, Papillons and a Bedlington Terrier. However, she has still to show her three favourite breeds, the Wire Fox Terrier, the Field Spaniel and the Irish Wolfhound. She likes these breeds because the Terrier is friendly and smart looking, the Spaniel has a good working nature and the Wolfhound is a gentle giant.

Dress Sense

Katie likes to wear a smart trouser suit with flat-soled shoes and she always ties her hair back to stop it getting in the way.

Achievements

Katie has collected a total of 34 semi-final qualifications for Richmond and has been 3rd twice and 5th twice in the semi-finals. She has been to the Scottish Junior Handler of the Year final and came fourth in 2000.

In addition to other placings, she has been the Best Border Terrier Handler at the Northern Border Terrier Club Championship in 1996 and 2000 and at the open shows in 1997, 1999, 2000 and 2001.

Memorable Moments

Her most memorable occasion so far has to be when she bred her first litter. There were no complications and her bitch produced three males and one female. Her family kept the female and called her Cally.

The most humorous situation she has ever come across is very familiar to most handlers. She was handling at an Exemption show, and together with all the other competitors in the class, watched a young boy of about five years old struggling to hold his dog, which was a German Shepherd!

When he had to do an Up and Down, disaster struck. He started out well, but then the dog noticed his owner and made straight for him, taking the little boy with him. The dog dragged the boy across the field and under the rope – but the boy then picked himself up and went back into the ring!

Her friends are very supportive towards Katie's hobby and they love her dogs. Some of them even go to the shows with her to watch. The ringcraft classes she attends do not hold a separate time for juniors but, nevertheless, she thoroughly enjoys them.

Top Tip

What Katie enjoys most is the tingly feeling she gets just before going into the ring but she generally loves everything about handling because it's fun and exciting. She just dislikes having to wait for classes when they are running late; by the time they are on, her dogs are tired and so is she. Her top tip is to never give up, whether you are placed first or last.

CHAPTER TEN

The World Show: A Personal Experience

This show is held over four days in different places throughout the world every two years. My prize for winning the Pedigree Chum Junior Handler of the Year title in January 1998 was a trip for two to the World Show in Helsinki, Finland plus £150 spending money.

I was asked by Liz Cartledge, the Hon. Secretary and joint founder of the Junior Handling Association, and an international judge, to choose which eight different breeds I would like to handle over the four days. This meant that I had to gain a first place on one of the days in the 11-17 age group to get through to the final on the last day. I chose two breeds for each day.

However, some time later, before the show closing date, I was informed that the runner-up, Helena Hutchings, and I had been invited to compete straight into the final on the last day. This was great news as it took the pressure off qualifying.

My Handling Choice

My first choice for that day had been the Afghan and this was accepted as my breed. I then had to concentrate on finding out all about handling an Afghan in more detail.

I needed 'hands-on' experience so I arranged to meet a Scottish Afghan breeder and exhibitor at her local dog training classes in Dundee in order to gain some knowledge and practical help. Using one of her Afghans, I had to learn how to groom the dog properly, move at the correct pace, get a feel for his size and shape, and pose him correctly.

As the June date for the Show approached, I felt confident that I knew as much as I possibly could about the Afghan Hound and I now wanted to put the knowledge into action.

The Journey

My dad and I flew from Aberdeen to Heathrow early on a Wednesday morning. We soon met up with Helena Hutchings and her mother, Jenny, at Heathrow, and then with Liz and Ferelith Somerfield, an international judge and editor-in-chief of *Dog World*, who were accompanying us on the flight to Helsinki.

My first impression of Finland was the abundance of trees and lakes, the weather was warm and Helsinki airport was very clean with a variety of super shops. We stayed in a lovely Holiday Inn which was connected to the Centre where the show was being held.

The Show Setting

On the first day of the show while Liz and Ferelith went off to judge, Helena, Jenny, dad and I walked to the main ring where the Junior Handling was being staged. The ring itself was magnificent. A stunning, white-curtained backdrop, with stairs leading down through the middle, instantly caught my eye. The ring was also very large, with a bright green carpet surrounded by spectator stands.

Nearly 40 young handlers, aged between 10 and 17 years of age, filled the ring. Only the first place winner from each day's class would qualify for the final on the Sunday.

The show itself reminded me very much of Crufts but had fewer trade stands. There were also many unusual breeds that I didn't recognise but, by the end of the four days, I had discovered more about them. The breed judging was very different from here in the UK, but it was interesting, because everyone in each class received a written critique of their dog after the judging of each class. Although there were many visitors, exhibitors and 15,000 dogs, the whole venue was kept remarkably clean.

Preparing For The Final

Because Helena and I, together with four other competitors from around the world had, as main winners from our respective countries, been invited to compete only in the final on the Sunday, this meant that we could relax and enjoy our holiday while waiting for the show's climax.

Then Sunday suddenly loomed ahead and I had to start thinking about the competition itself. Although I knew I would be handling an Afghan, it was not until 11am on the Sunday morning that I first encountered my lovely three-year-old bitch called "Tosca". I quickly built up a rapport with her in our junior room, close to the main ring. To let Tosca feel happy with me, I walked her around the show, giving encouraging words and I groomed her all over.

The Final

At about 3:45pm, the 10 junior finalists were called together and put in judging order behind the

The final line-up of the show.

scenes. At this point I was getting very excited as it was the first time I had ever handled an Afghan in competition. Tosca was waiting calmly, but I knew as soon as I went into the ring she would burst into life. It was an incredible atmosphere, hundreds of spectators, lights and an enthusiastic commentator. Helena and I hugged each other for good luck as we were both representing Great Britain.

The junior handling ring procedure was very much the same as in the UK; the judge, Graeme Missen, from Australia gave us normal breed patterns. Tosca coped well with all the distractions around and I had learned from her that she responded well to very gentle handling.

After we had all been seen, we were asked to leave the ring. This was the most anxious moment in the whole trip, as only a winner and a runner-up would be chosen. I have to admit I was a little confused because I was finding some difficulty understanding the commentator's instructions to the competitors and at one point I thought I had been eliminated.

The Winning

Suddenly, while we all waited nervously behind the scenes, the runner-up from Finland was announced and she ran into the ring, being greeted with much applause from the home crowd. Everything went quiet as we all listened intently to the final build-up by the Finnish commentator. She then announced that the winner came from Great Britain! My name was called and I couldn't believe it. Tosca sensed my

Marina, the proud winner of the finals. Photo: David Dalton.

joy as she also bounced into the ring. The press swooped upon us and I have to say it was the most exciting moment of my life.

At that minute I just wished that my mother, who had trained and coached me since I was six years old, could have been there to share my excitement. Poor mum couldn't have coped with the plane journey. However, I did manage to phone her from the show and I could hear her literally jumping up and down with joy at the news.

The trip as a whole was a fantastic experience – meeting new people, seeing new places, travelling and generally having fun.

CHAPTER ELEVEN

Junior Handling Judges

There is a danger that far too many judges are being appointed to adjudicate at Junior Handling because of their breed knowledge, without any consideration being given as to whether they have a true understanding of Junior Handling. The fault lies with the judges who make the wrong decision about taking up the appointment. They need to ask themselves one specific question: "Do I know anything about Junior Handling?"

It is so very unfair on those youngsters who train every week to improve their skills and performance, to then be judged poorly at the weekend. A Junior Handling specialist would not go and judge an Obedience competition just because of his or her dog knowledge. In my experience, over the years, I have found that the best judges are those that have come through the Junior Handling ranks themselves, or have handled at top level breed competition.

The Handler: **Alex Paisey**

Alex lives in Swansea, Wales, and is involved with almost everything doggy related. He primarily shows a Deerhound in Junior Handling competition but has also shown a Belgian Shepherd Dog (Tervueren), Miniature Long haired Dachshunds, Retrievers (Golden and Flat coated), Cocker Spaniel, Whippet and an Afghan Hound. He has also shown dogs outside the UK and handled a Lagotto Romagnolo at a European show.

It all began when he first attended KCJO camp with his brother Philip (another successful ex-junior handler) when he was six years old. He started off with a Miniature Long-haired Dachshund puppy and then, as both his ability and skill began to appear, he was hooked! For several years he has also been a KCJO scout at Crufts.

Alex has shown dogs outside the UK; here, he is handling a Lagotto Romagnolo in Luxembourg.

The Group: **Hound Group**

Hunting breeds which are split into two different categories: sight hounds (Greyhound, Afghan, Borzoi, Irish Wolfhound) and scent hounds (Beagle, Bloodhound, Basset Hound).

The Breed: **Deerhound**

Showing style: ***Floor Dog***
When presenting, the Deerhound must free stand and Alex holds the head for support. The Deerhound must never be strung up. The feet should be placed four-square and be checked all the time as with a tall breed it is often difficult to notice a paw out of place. This breed moves at a moderate graceful pace and is not baited, as the ears should lie flat. But Alex says that an occasional treat is acceptable as praise after the dog has completed his round. The dog should be bathed four to five days before the show in order to allow the coat to settle. At the show, the coat should be groomed without stripping out the normal double

The tall, noble Deerhound is the breed with which Alex is most experienced.

coat. There should be a natural ruff at the neck and this should be simply tidied up, using a comb. The ears and feet should be checked for stray hairs and nails should be trimmed without losing the usual curve.

Other Favourites

Apart from the dogs Alex lives with, his favourite three breeds are the Border Terrier, the Belgian Shepherd Dog (Tervueren) and the Irish Wolfhound. He explains that the Border is friendly and lovely to show, the BSD is a striking looking dog with a great temperament and the Wolfhound is a gentle giant.

Dress Sense

When he competes against other handlers, Alex wears a black or white shirt with beige trousers and a red patterned tie. On his feet, he wears black hard-soled shoes.

Achievements

Alex has achieved much success as a Junior Handler in Britain as well as representing the UK abroad. His most significant win was the Richmond Hound 6-11 years class which enabled him to compete in the Pedigree Chum Junior Handler of the Year in 1998. This win was extra special as he was handling a borrowed Dachshund. Frequent wins at Open and Championship level, with both his own dogs and with borrowed dogs, has helped Alex gain the confidence to show many more breeds for years to come.

Memorable Moments

He recalls that on one occasion, when he was just starting out, the judge had asked him to do a Reverse Triangle and then an Up and Down. He completed the Triangle fine but then forgot to do the Up and Down! Another humorous experience was trying to persuade a seven year old Deerhound to do a T without taking half-an-hour over it!

His school friends are not that bothered about his interesting hobby although they do make a fuss when they want him to go out and he is off to a show instead. Sometimes it is difficult to persuade his school headmaster to get time off for events like Crufts, so Alex hardly ever attends mid-week shows during school time. He does attend ring craft classes to train his young Deerhound and also to help other juniors.

Top Tip

Alex loves the social scene in handling but also thinks it's great when you win and you don't expect to! He really doesn't like Junior Handling judges who don't know what they are looking for in a good handler and some even forget that you are there. He also disapproves of the fact that some show societies do not allow adequate warning when the classes are about to be judged (held in lunch breaks).

His essential piece of advice is always to keep one eye on the judge.

JUDGING JUNIOR HANDLERS

Judges must assess the handlers, not the dogs.

Some young handlers need gentle encouragement from the judge if they are inexperienced.

Indeed, I was at one show where the Junior Handling judge came back very late from lunch and promptly went to sleep at the judges' table while the handlers were assembling in the ring. This sets a truly bad example to everyone in and around the ringside.

As another example, I overheard the judge asking her steward "So what do I have to do then?" I have only one word for this – 'unprofessional'.

Judging The Judge

These are the main questions that any person who has been invited to judge Junior Handling classes should ask themselves.

1. **Have I ever handled a dog before in Junior Handling or breed classes?**

2. **If I accept this appointment, can I afford to do it in an Honorary capacity or do I need payment?**

3. **Am I physically fit enough to carry out the judging?**

4. **Am I the right age to deal with the appointment?**

5. **Would I be able to give up a whole day for this appointment (if not judging anything else)?**

6. **Have I a nice, friendly attitude towards young people?**

7. **Do I understand the technical patterns?**

8. **Do I know about the Golden Rule?**

9. **Would I recognise the rapport between handler and dog?**

10. **Could I deal with any safety issues within the ring, such as dogs fighting?**

11. **Would I be able to set an example on dress presentation myself?**

12. **Am I prepared to write and send a critique of the classes following judging?**

If you have said 'yes' to all these questions then, in my mind, you would be the ideal Junior Handling judge.

Good Judging Tips

- It is sometimes a nice idea to take with you two small gifts for the two winning handlers as a momento of the occasion.

- Remember not to give the younger age group class too many difficult tasks or patterns to complete, as the younger handlers don't have as much experience as those in the older class.

- At most, give handlers in the 6-11 years age group a 'circle altogether at the start', then individually a 'reverse triangle' and 'twice up and down'.

- For the more mature and experienced handlers in the 12-16 years age group, ask all the handlers to go around the ring twice. On the second turning circle, move to the edge of the ring so all the handlers have to change hands.

- Individually, ask each handler to perform a letter T or letter L. Also ask them to then go Up and Down once and change from your original position.

- To find the Best Junior Handler, ask the two class winners to go Up and Down together, to achieve some variation. If it is really difficult to decide between the two, try asking specific breed or anatomy questions.

Appendix: a sample entry form.

CLACKMANNANSHIRE CANINE CLUB
200 CLASS OPEN SHOW
(Will be held under Kennel Club Rules & Regulations)
17th NOVEMBER 2001
AT DEVONVALE EQUESTRIAN CENTRE, FISHCROSS, by ALLOA

You may enter all your breeds on one form.
Use a seperate form for each owner
Entries Close
Monday 6th November 2001
(Postmark)

ENTRY FEES	
First entry for each dog @ £2.50	*£2.50*
Subsequent entries with same dog @ £1.00	
Junior Handling entries @ £0.50	*£0.50*
Pre-paid Catalogues @ £2.00	
Adverts @ £10.00 / £6.00	
Membership £1.00 Per Person	
TOTAL CHEQUE, P. O., CASH	*£3.00*

INSTRUCTIONS This form must be used by one person only (or partnership). Writing MUST BE IN INK OR INDELIBLE PENCIL. Use one line only for esch dog. The name of the dog and all the details as recorded with the Kennel Club must be given on this entry form. If an error is made the dog may be disqualified by the Committee of the Kennel Club. All dogs must be REGISTERED at the Kennel Club and if a Registered dog has changed ownership the TRANSFER must be registered before the date of the Show. A puppy under 6 months old cannot be exhibited.

	REGISTERED NAME OF DOG Put NAF/TAF if Applicable	BREED	SEX D or B	Full Date of Birth	BREEDER If Owner put "OWNER"	SIRE	DAM	Classes to be numerically
	BELSMARD TENDER KISS ATC No.:	*BEAGLE*	*B*	*19/10/99*	*OWNER*	*CRAIGMOUNT BEN BHREAC*	*BELSMARD DOUBLE KISS*	
	ATC No.:							
	ATC No.:							

* The Kennel Club Authority to Compete number for dogs resident outside the U.K. must be stated or the entry will be returned.

JUNIOR HANDLERS NAME: *MARINA WHITE* **AGE:** *16*
JUNIOR HANDLERS NAME: **AGE:**

DECLARATION CHECK ALL DETAILS ARE CORRECT BEFORE POSTING

I/We agree to submit to and be bound by the Kennel Club Rules and Regulations in their present form or as they may be ammended from time to time in relation to all canine matters with which the Kennel Club are concerned.

I/We also undertake to abide by the Regulations of the Show and not to bring to the Show any dog which has contracted or been knowingly exposed to any infections or contagious disease during the twenty one days prior to the day of the Show.

Any dog which I/We exhibit will only be prepared for exhibition in accordance with the requirements of the Kennel Club Regulations for the Preparation of Dogs for Exhibition F (B).

I/We further declare that, I/We believe to the best of my/our knowledge that the dogs are not liable to disqualification under Kennel Club Regulations.

Usual Signature of owner(s) ---------------------------- Date *6/10/01*

NOTE: Dogs entered in breach of Kennel Club Show Regulations are liable to disqualifications whether or not the owner was aware of the breach

Name of owners Mr/Mrs/Miss
Address *88 JOE BLOGGS STREET*
DOGGYTOWN
BARKSHIRE Postcode
Telephone *(01234) 000000*
All entries and fee which should be PREPAID to:
CHEQUES AND P. O.'s TO BE MADE PAYABLE TO C. C. C.

Useful Addresses

THE KENNEL CLUB:

1-5 Clarges Street
London
W1Y 8AB
http://www.the-kennel-club.org.uk
General Enquiries 0208 629 5828

Kennel Club Junior Organisation (KCJO)

0208 493 6651 Ext. 230
Address for KCJO same as above.

Junior Handling Association (J.H.A)

Mrs Liz Cartledge
Ryslip Kennels
Church Lane
Binfield
Nr. Bracknell
Berks
Telephone: 01344 424144

Dog Newspapers

Dog World
Somerfield House
Wotton Road
Ashford
Kent
TN23 6LW
Telephone: 01233 621877
http://www.dogworld.co.uk

Our Dogs
5 Oxford Road Station Approach
Manchester
M60 1SX
Editorial telephone: 0161 228 1984
Advertising telephone: 0161 236 2660
http://www.ourdogs.co.uk

Glossary

About Turn	Mostly used when joining two patterns together
Agility	A canine sport where dogs have to negotiate certain obstacles.
Bait	Food used to encourage a dog to obey commands
Benching	A way of securing dogs which is used at most Group and General Championship Shows
Best In Show (BIS)	The exhibit which has been beaten by no other dog at the show
Best Junior Handler	The handler who has won his class and then beaten the other class winners

Bite	The relative position of the upper and lower teeth when the dog's mouth is closed
Breed Record Holder	A dog who has been awarded the most Challenge Certificates in his breed
Breed Showing	Competitions where the dog is being judged, not the handler
Breed Standard	A description of a breed's ideal dog, against which all dogs of that breed are judged
Catalogue	A list of all the entries in a show in their respective classes
Challenge Certificate (CC or ticket)	Awarded to the best dog and best bitch of each breed in the show. Only given at Championship Shows

Champion/ Show Champion	Title awarded to a dog which has gained three CCs under three different judges
General Championship Show	The highest level of all-breed dog show, which can be held over 2, 3 or 4 days to accommodate the volume of entries
Group Championship Show	A high level show limited to just one group and held on one day only
Changing hands	Used when the handler has to manoeuvre the dog from his right side to the left, or vice versa
Charge	Another term for dog
Closing date	The last date by which an entry can be received and entered by the show secretary
Critique	A written assessment by

the judge of the class which has been judged. It reports and explains the placings. Critiques are sent to *Dog World* and *Our Dogs* for publication.

Crufts Established in 1886 and held once a year. Crufts is the largest dog show in the world, attracting the top 20,000 dogs in the UK and now, with the relaxation of the quarantine rules, dogs world-wide.

Dog show Where dogs are shown to be judged, with the aim of winning through to become Best Exhibit in Show (BIS)

Exemption A low level type of show, normally with about four to eight pedigree classes and some novelty classes

Exhibit	A dog entered at a show
Exhibitor	The owner or handler of a dog
Flews	The dog's lips
Floor dog	Large dogs which are individually assessed when standing on the floor
Four-square	The position of the dog's paws
Free-standing	The handler stands in front of the dog and does not hold the dog in any way
Gait	The dog's movement
Going over	The judge assesses a dog by feeling his body
Golden Rule	The handler must not get in between the dog and the judge

Group	A collection of various breeds of dogs which share the same characteristics
Line-up	The class of handlers and their dogs position themselves in a continuous line around the edge of the ring
Loose lead	The lead is slackened to allow the dog to move freely. It is the opposite of 'strung-up'
Obedience	A form of competition which tests the dog's ability to obey commands
Pace	The speed at which the dog should be gaited
Patterns	Compulsory movements when competing in Junior Handling
Placing	Awards from first to fifth place

Presentation	The way the handler is dressed
Presenting	Stacking or free-standing the dog to the judge
Puppy	A dog up to 12 months of age
Rapport	The relationship and bond between dog and handler
Ring	The area, which is normally square or oblong shaped, where the class takes place
Ring number	Each competitor is assigned a number which should be worn in the ring during the competition
Ring craft classes	Places where enthusiasts can train their dogs for the show ring
Rocking	The term used to describe a dog which leans back on its hind legs

Schedule A list of the classes, judges and breeds for a show, and necessary for entry to a show

Schooled A dog trained for the show ring

Set up Positioning a dog into his appropriate stance

Shadowing As a judge walks around a dog, so the handler is required to move in order to avoid breaking the Golden Rule

Show pose The handler should show the dog in his most natural state

Stacking The dog's head and/or tail has to be held for the show pose

Stewarding This includes such duties as collecting handlers at

	the start of a class, marking down absentees, recording the winners and handing out rosettes
Tight (taut) lead	Used when moving or standing, so that the dog's head is firmly under control
Table dog	Small dogs which are individually assessed when standing on a table
The Kennel Club (KC)	Founded in 1873, it is the ultimate arbiter of the dog world, classifying breeds, registering pedigree dogs, giving awards and promoting the improvement of dogs
Titbits/Treats	Used in the training of dogs as a reward and as a way of keeping a dog's attention properly focussed

Turns	A movement crucial to the successful completion of any pattern
Veteran	A dog aged over seven years

Index

A

B

C

H

I

J

K

L

M

N

O

P

Q

R

S

T

U

V

W